My Barefoot Journey

My Barefoot Journey

Memories of
ALFRED H. "SMOKEY"
PHILLIPS

by

ALFRED H. PHILLIPS
and his son BOB

3

SILVER SPRUCE PUBLISHING
FLAGSTAFF, ARIZONA

Silver Spruce Publishing

2218 E. Cedar Ave, Flagstaff, AZ 86004

Printed in the United States of America

First Printing: March 2007

10 9 8 7 6 5 4 3 2

ISBN 978-0-945188-02-5
ISBN 0-945188-02-1

Library of Congress Control Number
2007901198

This book is dedicated to my grandchildren:

Brian, Amy, Kristen, Amanda, Kyle and Ryan

Acknowledgements

Paying tribute to all the wonderful people that helped me put this book together would fill up many volumes and even then I would probably forget someone very important. I suppose that the most important person to thank would be my Father since he lived it. In retelling the story I must include my Mother. She helped him when I first convinced him to attempt putting the story together and assisted Ann and I when it was first being typed. Others that must be included: Ann Phillips, my wife for doing the initial transcription; Harry Bailey and Sue Holsomback for typesetting the final manuscript; Phil Rulon for his research advice as well as for the incredible help in not only proofreading but also book design etc.; Curt Rulon for his invaluable assistance in the genealogy areas; I also must thank Sylvia and Bill Neely for lending their expert opinions on the way to present the story. My sister and brother-in-law Jane and Tommy Robbins also helped with some of the historical aspects of the family. I also owe a debt of gratitude to my son Eric Phillips and the staff at Mirror Images Printing. They put the whole thing on paper. I am most grateful also for the help of the fine people at the Kansas Children's Service League. Without the help of people like these whole project would not have been possible and I can only say, Thank You.

Foreword

My Father was named Alfred Herman Phillips. He was known throughout his young years as Smokey and in his later life he was known as Fred. I always knew him as Dad and for purposes of this story that is how I will refer to him.

It is not my intention to rewrite Dad's autobiography. I am very pleased that I was instrumental in convincing him to write an account of his life and rewriting his work would take away much of the flavor of the story. My plan is to flesh out some of the parts of the story which I feel are important and Dad did not, for one reason or another, want to put in the book.

At the time I started to work on Dad to write his memoirs he was over 75 years old. His mind was clear and his memory was excellent. Although he always said that he had never done anything of importance that would warrant his putting it down on paper we finally convinced him to do it by reminding him that he would probably be dead before his grandchildren could hear his "first liar ain't got a chance tales." No one could have possibly guessed that by the time he passed his grandchildren would be grown men and women with children of their own. I also told him that even though he never thought that he had done anything important it was a fact that he had lived through a fantastic period of history that stretched all the way from the horse and buggy to space travel. I believe it's important for his descendants to understand what life was like for people in the early part of the twentieth century. Believing that he was writing this story for young children he left out some things that would be interesting to a more adult audience.

In researching this book I was amazed at how accurate Dad's memory was throughout the entire manuscript. His ability to remember times, dates and sequences of occurrence was phenomenal especially considering the fact that he had no easily available source of reference except what he remembered. Dad kept no journals or diaries at any time to my knowledge, so he really could only rely on his truly incredible memory. It also must be remembered that Dad wrote this autobiography in 1972 thru 1974. Computers, even if they would have been available, were not an option.

Throughout the book it is my plan to leave Dad's writing in straight type and my contribution in italics.

Interested readers should access the Internet via Google and enter "Remount Depots during WW1" for a look into Army life during World War1 through Dad's eyes.

Bob Phillips

Book One

Early Days

1896 - 1907

In starting this story I am going back a long time, to about the turn of the century or before –

ST. LOUIS, MISSOURI
1896 - 1903

I was born April 4th, 1896 in St. Louis, Missouri. However there is no record in the office of statistics. In those days births were seldom recorded, as most children were born at home and brought into the world by a midwife. Only the wealthy could afford to go to the hospital and have a doctor's care. As it is my birth was never recorded.

I can barely remember my father. My mother told me that he died about the time that they started to build the St. Louis World Fair Buildings. His name was Louis and by occupation he was a house painter and paperhanger. In those days rooms were decorated by having the walls and ceilings papered with a decorative paper and it was quite an art to put this on so that it looked nice. After my Father passed away my Mother remarried in 1903, early in the year. This time she married a man who came here from Germany. In fact my Mother was born in Berlin, Germany. His name was Mike Dauner. Mr. Dauner's home was in a small town in southern Oklahoma – Lawton.

LAWTON, OKLAHOMA
1903 - 1907

The country was just then opening up. The town site was laid out and the lots numbered. Any one wishing a lot bought a number. At the time Oklahoma was territory and as such was under federal control. The government sold the lots and a drawing was held. If I remember my history, it seems as if they issued lot numbers and sold them. You paid for a number, then reached in a box or bowl and picked out a number. The planners had a town site plotted. The lots were numbered. Whatever number you had would match a lot number. That lot was yours. At any rate his lot later became well situated in regards as to how the town developed.

Mr. Dauner got a good lot in a location that later became part of the business part of town. At first he just built a small shack or cabin. As I look back over the years I imagine it was probably 14' x 14' with a flat cabin type roof. This was set rather well back in the lot. Later he built a larger building near the street, a two story building covered with corrugated iron. There was an inside stairway leading up from the street. There was also a stairway leading up from the backyard. The back stairway was built up on the outside of the building with an outside landing at the rear end of the hall. Downstairs on the ground level was not finished. In the upstairs part of the house there were four rooms, a hallway, and the stairway that led to the street.

I don't know how he and mother met, but they were married in St. Louis. He took us to Lawton. I seem to remember we went there in March 1903. At first we lived in the shack. Then we moved upstairs.

I forgot to mention that the downstairs of this building was not finished as a dwelling for some time as I believe he had intended to open a shop of some sort there. He also dug a well in the backyard. Mother used the small place as a washhouse and storeroom.

Lawton at that time was just emerging from the rag town stage or tent town. The town was small. There were no sidewalks or made streets, no sewers, and no city water. Most buildings were lumber or frame. We happened to have one of the few water wells in town. Most people bought water. Water was hauled in barrels in a wagon and sold by the gallon, or maybe five gallons. I don't remember, but I do remember seeing water delivered in barrels and sold door to door. Some of the folks in the neighborhood got water from our well. However I don't recall Mr. Dauner charging them for it.

As Lawton was laid out the streets were numbered from east to west, and named alphabetically from north to south – A, B, C, D, etc. We lived on E Street between 4th and 5th. As I mentioned before there were no sidewalks as such at that time. Oh, some people haphazardly made a boardwalk in front of their places, especially business houses. As I said there were not water works so we had to carry all our water from the well. We did have a hand pump to get the water out of the well. Mother had a five gallon lard can on a low bench in the kitchen, besides two

Annie 13   Elizabeth 12
Dad's sisters

buckets and it was my job to keep that can and the buckets full of water.

As for fuel for cooking and heating we used wood. We had a box behind the stove in the kitchen and I had to keep it filled. I also had to keep mother supplied with water and wood when she washed.

As I mentioned we had no sewers. But we had a little building on the rear of the lot we used as a toilet. We also had a milk cow and barn on the rear of the lot. I remember the cow hated me and I stayed clear of her.

Every day before I left the house I had to wash the morning dishes. Also, as I said I filled the wood box and water can and buckets. This I had to do. Once I started school I had to do these chores before and after school. I can't remember when I didn't do dishes, even when I had to stand on a low bench or box to be able to reach. We had no sink, so I had to use a dishpan on the kitchen table. I had to heat the water in a teakettle on the stove. After the dishes were washed I would pour the dirty dish water in a bucket called the slop bucket. Then carry it away back in the backyard and dump it.

When we wanted to bathe mother would build a fire in the stove in the shack and heat the water. Then she would put me in a round washtub and scrub me.

In the fall of 1903 I started to school. By that time Lawton had two schools. They were situated in the block between 4th and 5th North boundary (one block north of A) and A. The buildings were frame and in the shape of a cross. One building was from 1st to 4th grade and the other was 5th to 8th grade. By then I was seven years old and entered the 1st grade. We had homemade desks and benches. Four kids sat together a boy, a girl, a boy and a girl. I guess that was a good idea, as I imagine the idea had an effect to keep us in line. I can't imagine what four boys in a seat would do. However it did sort of embarrass both boys and girls.

There were several other boys about my age in the neighborhood. I do remember the names of two of them, Bus Crisp and Lynn Price. I don't seem to remember the others.

We had not been in Lawton but a few days and I had as yet seen no Indians. Lawton was full of them so one day I was running around with some other kids (I don't remember if it was one of the above or not). We were exploring an old house. When I came around the corner I came face to face with a big buck Indian. They were blanket Indians those days. They all wore blankets and went barefooted, the hottest summer or coldest winter days. However when I saw this big buck Indian he scared the devil out of me. Boy I left there, and I went for home in a hurry. After a while the other kids came to me and asked why I left in such a hurry. I said, didn't you see that big old Indian? They laughed at me and told me that they were tame and would not hurt me. But it still took me a long while before I would trust them.

In 1904 my oldest sister was born. They named her Annie. I don't remember what month. Then in 1906 by younger sister, Elizabeth was born, and again I don't remember what month.

In those days all of us kids went barefoot in the summer. In fact I went barefoot every summer until I was 15 years old. I got one pair of shoes a year and they had to last from late fall to early spring. By spring they usually were ready to fall off my feet. About 1904 there commenced to be some board sidewalks around town. As to be expected I got my share of splinters and bruises from being barefoot.

Getting back to Indians, there were two old timers in the country, also two tribes, the Apache and the Comanche. Geronimo was chief of the Apache. They had him at Fort Sill under military guard. Everywhere he went two U. S. soldiers guarded him. Every three months the Indians were paid a certain sum of money by the government, a sort of indemnity. On those days the town would be full of Indians of both tribes. There was a building down the street that was the old Keegan Hotel. It had a long porch with a railing and benches. They would bring Geronimo there and hold him on those days. We kids would go by and salute him by saying, "Hi, Hi John". In fact we addressed all Indians by that means. When we said Hi, Hi to him he would answer the same way so I can truthfully say I have talked to Geronimo and he has talked to me however our conversation was rather limited.

The rumor got out among us kids that he had a blanket made of human scalps and had 99 scalps in it. He wanted one more scalp to make an even 100. None of us was anxious to be the 100th victim.

Geronimo was a short pudgy guy, maybe 5 foot 6 inches tall, ugly flat faced. I heard later that he died in 1910 and was buried at Fort Sill. And in a few days his grave was found opened and his body gone. No doubt his people moved him to some secret spot. The whereabouts may never be known. Incidentally he was captured in Arizona in 1886 near the Mexican border. I believe by the 6th U.S. Cavalry. He and his followers were sent to Florida, where they lost a lot of them. They were desert Indians and of course Florida swamps were too wet for them. They brought what was left of them back to Fort Sill and put them on a reservation in the Wichita Mountains.

The other chief was Quanah Parker. He was head of the Comanche. He was somewhat taller than Geronimo, more thin and sharp featured. He could talk English very good. I really don't know if Geronimo could speak English or not. Quanah Parker's mother was a white woman. She was captured in west Texas when she was a small girl and raised Indian. Her name was Cynthia Ann Parker. She later married an Indian. The Comanche had their reservation on the west end of the Wichita Mountain range.

Bus Crisp's parents had a small house in the rear of their home and Quanah Parker rented that and stayed there when in town for their pay. He had two wives. He owned what at that time was called a hansom cab. It was a closed in vehicle. Very much like a coupe, only it was drawn by horses. It had doors on the side. The seats were cross ways and faced each other. The driver sat outside and his seat was high enough so he could look back over the top of the cab. He usually had four horses hitched to it, two on the tongue at the wheels and two in the lead. They were small Indian ponies. They always had a bunch of dogs with them. When they came to town we always could expect a few good dogfights, as the town dogs would want to fight the Indian dogs.

As before stated, Quanah Parker could talk good English when he wanted to. However at times when he did not want to be bothered he would not talk to us. He would merely tell us to "Go, go – No savvy". Then we knew we had better take out, as the tone of his voice was enough to tell us we were not welcome. Most times he was very friendly. I don't know when he died or where he is buried.

As I look back over the years it seems to me I was no worse or no better than other kids my age. But like all kids I could get into trouble.

I mentioned that we lived upstairs in the house and there was a rear stairway that had a landing about 4 feet by 4 feet at the top. The house door opened in. The screen door opened out. As I said before when mother was washing she usually did her baking. In those days one could not buy bread or cookies in a store or bakery. That was done at home. One-day mother had made her bread into loaves and had put them in pans waiting for the right time to put them in the oven. She told me to bring the pan of bread downstairs to put in the oven. It must have been cool weather because the inner door was closed. I went into the kitchen picked up the pan with the loaves in and got out on the porch landing OK, but to close the door I had to put the pan down. I sat the pan on the corner of the railing around the landing and turned and closed the door. As I turned back to the bread one of my cronies called to me and waved. I waved back striking the bread pan and tipping it off the railing down into the yard below. Well the yard was covered with coal cinders and the bread landed upside down. Mr. Dauner had gotten some cinders from the railroad to put in the yard, so the yard would not be so muddy in wet weather. Mother really worked me over for that.

Another time I got into trouble; in those days small pox was a disease they had not gotten control of as yet, however they were working on it. My friend, Lynn Price, lived just two doors from us and he contracted small pox. As soon as it was known Mother told me to stay away from there. I had not seen Lynn in a couple of days. I happened to look over that way and I could see him through the window of his house. Mother happened to be away from home that afternoon. I thought I would go over and talk to him through the window. After I got there and talked to him he said come on in, I am about well. He was right in the peeling stage. I went in, but I didn't stay long as I saw my mother returning home. I tried to slip out before she saw me, but I didn't make it. When I got home I really got a licking. Also I was taken to the doctor's office and vaccinated. I had to be vaccinated the third time before it took.

Another time I got into trouble, I was all dressed up one Sunday and sent off to Sunday school. A Christian church was not far from where we lived. I seem to remember that Mother was a Lutheran, but she always seen that I went to some Sunday school. At any rate as I said, I was all dressed up nice – coat and pants. We all wore short knee length pants those days with long black stockings, usually held up by elastic garters. (When not tied up with a strip of torn rag.) However this particular Sunday I met some other kids and we decided to play hooky, and do something more exciting than go to church. Hooky is called ditching now. There was a cotton oil mill in the southeast section of town. One of the gang suggested we go down there and play in the cottonseed, so we did. The seed pile was real high and there was a walk above it. We would climb up the walk and jump off into the seed. It was real fun. But when it came time to go home, my clothes were white with cotton lint and the material of my clothes was such that I could not get it off. As usual I got it good, not only for the condition of my clothes but also for playing hooky from church.

It was about five blocks to school. I usually went east to 4th Street and then north to A Street. At times I used to meet a man who became well known, a Senator Thomas P. Gore, one of Oklahoma's early territorial lawmakers. He was blind or nearly so. I would meet him at the corner of 4th Street and E Street. He must have had an office somewhere on C Street, as he would always leave me there. He was a short man, always wore the conventional black suit and black hat, as worn by lawyers and politician of the time. I remember him very well.

There was another character there at the time called Heck Thomas. Mr. Thomas was supposed to be a Deputy U.S. Marshal. He was a big man, tall and heavy, or so it seemed to me. He always carried a big six-shooter on his hip. (However a lot of people carried guns those days, and not all of the guns could be seen.)

I would also meet him at times and walk along and talk to him. I would walk with him to the corner of 4th and D Streets. He would cross 4th and then go east on D Street. I remember one morning I was on my way to school and met him, and as usual he left me at 4th and D. I started north across D and he went east. It must have been in the winter as it was rather foggy. I had just about gotten across the street when I heard shooting. I looked and through the haze I could see Mr. Thomas fall to his hands and knees, at the same time try to pull his gun. In fact he did get his gun out and fired it towards a building. I later found out it was a door to a stairway leading into a building. It seems as if a man was standing in the door and shot Thomas as he was passing. I don't know how many shots were fired, but it seems as if a newspaperman by the name of Russell killed him.

At the time (about 1905 or 1906) Oklahoma was trying to become a state, and some factions wanted statehood and others did not. As I seem to remember along with statehood there was a rider, which would also bring prohibition along with statehood. This really happened when Oklahoma became a state in 1907. Oklahoma went dry at the same time.

In those days people took their politics seriously. Politicians were careful of what they said about their opponents. If they even hinted that their opponent was a liar they had to be able to prove it or fight.

I want to get a hold of an Oklahoma history and find out more about the above.

Another incident I remember very well happened thus. There was a blacksmith shop on the corner of 5th and E. Operated by a man by the name of Reed. I used to like to sit in the door and watch him work. In those days a blacksmith was a farrier (a person that shoes horses) as well. They had to make their horseshoes. Usually they kept horseshoes made ahead. Then all they had to do was shape the shoe to the horse's hoof.

One day I was over there and I was sitting on the ground in the edge of the doorway. The door way was large enough to drive a team and wagon through. Mr. Reed was making horseshoes. He had a piece of iron almost white hot and he had to cut off a piece of it. He cut it off on what is called a hardy. It is a triangular piece of iron that sticks up on the end of the anvil, and is sort of sharp on top. When a blacksmith wants to cut off a piece of iron he heats it real hot and then lays it on the hardy and hits it with his hammer, thereby cutting the iron where he wants.

At any rate Mr. Reed cut off this iron and a small piece approximately 1" x ¼" x ½" flew off and hit in the dust of the floor. (The floor of the shop was dirt.) When this small piece of iron (which was white hot) hit the dirt it turned almost the color of the dirt. About then a big Buck Indian walked into the shop and as I mentioned they were always barefooted. He did not see the hot iron and

25

he set his foot down on it. I got up on my feet and I wondered if he would ever feel that hot iron on his foot. To me it seemed a long time before it took effect, but when it did, that Indian let out a howl and ran over and stuck his foot in the slack tub (a tub of water beside the anvil, the smithy used to cool iron). I don't know if the iron stuck the bottom of his foot, but he reached down and felt his foot as if he was picking the iron out. It could very well have stuck as their feet had a very heavy callus.

Another thing we used to do was hunt beer and whiskey bottles. They were worth a penny apiece. And for a penny we could get a couple of sticks of candy or a couple of jawbreakers. However we had to take them to a saloon to sell them. As we were not allowed to go in the front doors, we would go to the rear. Rap on the door and usually a Negro swamper would take the bottles and give us our pennies.

In those days the saloons put out a free lunch. One could buy a nickel beer and get a nice sandwich thrown in. There was a choice of cheese, sliced beef, pork, chicken, or turkey with all the trimmings. We kids would try to talk the swamper out of a sandwich, sometimes we were successful.

At one place where we sold our bottles they had a couple of empty beer cases in the yard behind the saloon, where they stored the empties. There was board fence around the yard. The swamper would put the bottles back there. We found a board loose and we would wait until he got back in the saloon and then we would reach through the fence and steal them back with maybe a couple of others. Then take them to another place and sell them. After a while this swamper got wise and would not buy our bottles.

The first automobile I ever saw was about 1905. It was red. The rear seat was higher than the front so people riding back there could see over the head of the driver. I believe the engine was under the rear seat. And to start the engine one had to crank it on the side of the car.

Book Two

Orphan's Home

1907 - 1911

Christian Service League Orphanage – 1906
Wichita. Kansas

ORPHAN'S HOME
1907 - 1911

After my sisters were born things were not the same at home so in July 1907 I was sent to an orphan's home. As for Bus Crisp and Lynn Price I heard Bus got into trouble and spent some time in prison. I never again heard of Lynn Price.

One day a lady came to the house and Mr. Dauner and mother and she talked. When the lady left (her name was Miss Shelly) I went with her. She took me to a home for orphans in Wichita, Kansas.

I don't know why I was sent there only I remember mother told me it was for the best.

The organization that ran the orphan's home was called The Christian Service League. It was a sort of foster home office. There was one house where we older kids were kept. The others were put in foster homes.

There were about five boys and as many girls in the place where I stayed. It was managed by an old couple by the name of Hosford. I can't remember all the kid's names. Some of the boys were John Natteford, Leon Kellem, and Charley Sortor. I can't seem to remember the other boy's names. We were all about the same age. As far as the girl's names, they were Evangeline Natteford (John's sister), Laura and Rose Finley. That is all the girl's names I can remember.

Life was not too bad there. Oh, we had a certain amount of chores to do. They had a cow and we had to keep the cow's barn cleaned. Keep water and wood in the house and clean the yard, etc.

The house was way out in the southwest part of Wichita. In fact it was the last house on that street, with lots of open land to the south and west for us to roam around and play.

There was a place about a mile or so on further west called the sloughs. Lots of water though it wasn't very deep. There was lots of fish in these sloughs and we caught a lot of them, mostly catfish, buffalo and German carp. We kept the home supplied and also sold some now and then. We got a short length of 1 in. chicken wire and made a seine; with that we could catch all we could carry in about a half an hour before we found our chicken wire we had been catching them by hand. We would form sort of a half circle and drive them up in the weeds and fall down on them. We got the idea that if we could get the pitchfork (we had been using one to clean out the barn) we could catch them with that. Mr. Hosford would not let us have the fork so one day we caught the old man gone from home and we slipped the fork out. On our way to the sloughs was a cornfield. In our explorations we found out there was a watermelon patch in the field. After we got finished fishing (incidentally the pitchfork was really the thing to catch fish that day) we decided we would get us a couple of watermelons. On our way to and from the slough we followed a railroad track. We put our fork and sack with fish down on the embankment along side of the track and proceeded to slip through the cornfield to the melon patch. We were real busy looking for melons when one of us looked up and there came the farmer with a whip in his hand. Boy, we scattered like quail in every direction. We finally got back together and started looking for our fish and pitchfork. But it was getting late in the evening and we were supposed to be home by dark. We did not

34

find the fish or the fork and we knew we would be in trouble if the old man found out we took the fork without permission so we were very quiet about it that night. The next morning we cleaned the barn with a shovel thinking maybe the old man would not miss the fork. But he did. When he got ready to feed the cow hay he missed it so he got us all together and asked why we took the fork after he told us not to, also what became of it? We had to tell him the truth. He told us to go look for it. Well, we went back to where we thought it should be, but no luck. They all decided we should ask the farmer if he had found it. But no one wanted to go tell the farmer we were in his melon patch. As I was the smallest (I was about the same age, but smaller than the other kids) I should be the one to go so we went over to the gate were the road went up to the farmer's yard. The other kids would not go up to the house. As I went up to the farmer's house, the farmer came out and came down towards the gate. The other kids wanted to run but were afraid to. For that matter so was I afraid to run. However I did stand my ground and when the farmer came up to me he said what do you boys want? I said, we were the boys who were in his melon patch the evening before. I also explained about the fish and the pitchfork. He started to laugh. Well we all were relieved, as we all just knew we were in for a licking. He said he has not seen the fork. We were really scared kids when that farmer came down the road towards us. He looked 10 feet tall when I told him we were in his melon patch. However he told us when we wanted melons to come and see him and he would give us all we wanted. After that his melon patch held no interest for us. We started looking for another melon patch. We were restricted to the premises for about a week for losing the fork.

Our neighbor to the rear was a bachelor who lived by himself in a small house. He raised a nice garden. For some reason we did not like him. We were told to stay away from there and leave him alone. But like all kids when they don't like anyone they will find some way to torment that person. He had a new muskmelon patch and that was temptation. We planned some way to get some of those muskmelons. One day some of us seen him leaving home, to go to town. He had to cross a rather high railroad embankment and after crossing the railroad he would be out of sight of his garden. We all went out behind the barn and dared each other to go get a muskmelon. Now what we didn't know was that while we were hatching this plan the old man in charge of us was in the barn and could see us through the cracks in the boards. He heard every word we said. A couple of us slipped over in his melon patch and got a few melons. (There was no fence around the garden) We were going to sit down behind the barn and eat them. About the time we were ready to start eating the melons the old man stepped around the corner of the barn. He made us lay the melons down and then he took all five of us in the barn and took a harness strap to all of us. Then when the owner came home he made us all take the melons over and give them to him. That was worse than the licking.

I often these days think that it is too bad kids don't have the fun we had. Now, we did not think of taking those melons as stealing. And we had all learned how to pick melons, etc. without doing damage to the plants. I can't remember of ever thinking of vandalism. We usually always had to make our fun. We had no movies, radio, or T.V. We would go in to a corn patch when the corn was right. Get a few ears and take them down on a creek, pull the shuck back and clean out the silk. Then push the shuck up again. While some one else would build a fire. We would pack the ears in mud. After we got the fire just right with lots of nice coals we would roast the corn, also we liked sweet potatoes fixed that way. We were like all healthy kids we were always hungry.

THE WILLIAMS
1908

Well the time came when I was sent out for adoption. I had started to school in Wichita and went until about the first of February 1908. When I was sent to stay with some folks in the area of Deer Creek, Oklahoma, a man and his two old maid sisters took me in.

His one sister was named Mary. The other was called Kitty. Kitty was sort of sickly and she stayed in her room. May was the housekeeper. I called them Uncle Charlie and Aunt May. They lived on a farm about two miles north of Deer Creek, Oklahoma. I imagine they were all in their forties. I liked them, and maybe I would have stayed there except for unforeseen events. I will explain later.

I was given duties to perform. Regular responsibilities like doing chores, bringing in wood, water and feeding stock. I learned to milk cows and had that to do twice a day, cleaning out the barn and chicken house.

When spring came I was put to work in the fields, at first on a stalk cutter. (In the fall when the corn was cured. It was picked and the stalks left standing after all the corn was gathered. Stock was turned into the fields to pick what they would out of the fields. But that always left the old dead stalks standing. They had to be removed or cut up before planting time.) I took this stalk cutter drawn by two horses. It chopped these dead stalks down and cut them up so they could be plowed under.

Then came garden time. Planting garden, setting out onions, etc. so you see I was learning.

We had several horses and mules. I was given a pony to ride into town and run errands. I got to be a pretty good rider. However I was thrown off this pony several times. Sometimes he did not want to obey me and he would throw me off, but I would get back on him and I usually won out.

Before I get too far ahead of myself, the Williams started me off in school as soon as I got there. There were some bigger boys in school who always tried out new kids when they started in that school. They started picking on me. I took it for a while and commenced to get fed up with it.

One day one of these boys came up behind me and put his leg around my feet and shoved me to the ground. I fell on my face, as I did my hand fell on an old buggy spoke (spoke is part of a wheel). This spoke was about 16 or 18 inches long with a knob on the end. Well when I get up off the ground I had this spoke in my hand and I turned and swung. I caught this kid along the side of the head. He went down. Another big kid ran up and I asked him if he wanted some. But he ran in to the schoolhouse for the teacher. (We had a woman teacher at the time.) But by the time she got there this kid was up on his feet, crying. I still had the spoke in my hand. She asked this kid if he was hurt. He cried and said his head hurt. She looked him over and there was no blood so she told him he would be all right. She called us all in and wanted to know what was the story. Some of the smaller kids told her how these larger kids had been teasing and picking on me. She told me I should not hit people with clubs and let it go at that. Needless to day I was no longer picked on by that gang.

As I said before school was soon out and I went to work in the fields, but at that I had lots of free time.

There was a family near us by the name of Packard. Mr. Packard was called Wes. He and a brother had made the run in 1886 and got his farm (I am referring to the Oklahoma land rush in April 1886. When this area was settled.) The Packard's had several boys and we had great times together. Swimming and fishing in Deer Creek, which ran through the place.

Like any boy I could sort of upset Uncle Charlie at times, and he would really lay me out. However he never struck me. He would be giving me a bawling out and as he had false teeth, at times his upper plate would drop. Then he could not talk. He would just sputter and walk off. When I would see him again you wouldn't think anything had happened.

Early that spring we butchered a big hog mainly for lard. We rendered the fat for lard. The lean meat was trimmed and fried down. Then while the lard was still warm it was poured into two-gallon crocks. However the lean fried meat was first put in the crocks then covered with lard. This was one method used in those days to preserve meat, as we had no refrigerators. We had a sort of storehouse in the rear of the main house and there was a shelf. These crocks of meat and lard were placed on this shelf.

As I said before, growing healthy kids are always hungry. One day after the days get real warm I was in the storeroom, and I could smell the lard in these jars. (However they were well covered.) I got to thinking of how good that fried pork had smelled when it was fried down so I got a long stick and sharpened the end and got up on a box and lifted the cover. Stuck the pointed end of the stick in the jar and speared a nice piece of fried pork. I kind of shook the loose grease off of it. And ate it. It was sure good. To make a long story short, I worked on that jar all summer. As it happened when Aunt May got meat for our meals she started on the other end of the line so she did not know what was going on until along in the fall.

One day I heard her tell Uncle Charlie that she would have to start on the last jar and wondered if he would have a hog to kill by time it was finished. A few days later she said to Uncle Charlie, how much meat was in that last jar? Why? He said it was full. She told him there was only one piece of meat in the jar. Uncle Charley looked at me. When he did my looks gave me away. I had eaten that jar empty that summer.

That same year Aunt May raised a lot of turkeys. She said that was to be her Christmas money. When they got about as large as a large chicken, Uncle Charlie asked her to have one to eat. But she said, "Nothing doing", they were her Christmas money.

There was a patch of alfalfa growing near the house and it was full of grasshoppers. Turkeys like grasshoppers. One day Uncle Charlie was mowing this patch, he called me and told me to drive these turkeys down there to get those grasshoppers. I did as I was told. He went on mowing. He said, "Get these damned turkeys out of here. I think I have cut the legs off of some of them". Sure enough he had cut the legs off of five of them. Then he told me, I am going to give you Hell for driving them down there. But don't let it worry you. As this is the only way we will get to eat any of them. I only planned to get one or two. He told Aunt May that I must have of misunderstood his orders. I was supposed to have driven them out of the field instead of into the field. She surely did raise the roof. But we had nice fried turkey. Aunt May did not beat me, but she gave us both hell. She said he should

40

know enough to stop mowing until she could drive the turkeys out.

They had a big barn and with all the stock (horses and cows) it was quite a job to keep it clean and that was my job. Uncle Charlie had made a two-wheel cart with a box on to haul the dirt out. I used that to clean the barn and chicken house.

We had a team of gray horses. One of them didn't like me and got his bluff in on me so I would have to wait until his stall was empty before I could clean it. He would try to kick me every time I got near. However to feed him we had an aisle in front of them. When I would walk in front and feed them he would try to bite me. When Uncle Charlie was not around I carried a club and when he would try to bite me I would hit him across the side of the head. Maybe that is one reason why he hated me.

That summer they had a niece and nephew come out from Chicago for a visit. The boy's name was Paul Stetson (I believe). I don't remember the girl's name. At any rate Paul was about three or four years older than me. He started bossing me around and he didn't like it when Uncle Charlie would give him a job, and I would wind up doing it until Uncle Charlie got wise and laid the law down to him.

One day I was cleaning out the barn and Paul was told to clean out the chicken coop. I had the cart first and had it almost loaded when he came in the barn and told me he wanted the cart. I told him he could have it when I got through. He said he wanted it now and he tipped it over. It dumped right there on the barn floor. There was a ball peen hammer lying on a sill along the barn wall. I picked it up and threw it at him. Barely missing his head. It knocked a board loose on the wall of the barn. He left there in a hurry and he told Uncle Charlie. When Uncle Charlie got there he asked why I threw the hammer at him. I told him I was tired of him bossing me around and picking on me. I showed him where Paul had dumped the cart. He took Paul to the house. I don't for sure know what happened, but Paul left me alone after that.

As I said there was a bunch of Packard kids, four I believe. We would get together whenever we could. One day they came over and we started out across the field where there had been hay out. The hay had been stacked about in the center of the field. I don't know where we were going only that we were walking across the field. We came across a bumblebee nest so we decided to see if we could get some bumblebee honey. We went to the house and got a jug of water. Thinking we might drown the bees out, but that didn't work so some of us decided to try to burn them out. We piled dry straw on the nest and set it afire. Well we ended up burning the entire field as well as the stack of hay. Well the hay belonged to the Packard's, but Uncle Charlie had to pay $10.00 for my part in the affair. This happened in 1908.

Forty years later in 1948 mother, Bob and I stopped by there and saw Mrs. Packard. I told her who I was and we laughed about the haystack fire in which her boys and I were responsible. Uncle Charley, Aunt May, Aunt Kitty and Mr. Packard were long since passed away. However most of her boys were still living.

Uncle Charlie's health failed and he had to be operated on. I remember a doctor came out to the farm and he afterwards told me he was operated in, what was called in those days the parlor, on a large table. As he seen his health was bad they decided they could not keep me and they sent me back to the home. Mrs. Packard told me many years later he died of cancer. I really believe that had he not lost his health I would have had a good home with them. They were good to me.

I was sent back to the home the first part of November 1908. I remember it was the day Taft was elected President.

I almost over looked a very important event, which concerned me. Christmas 1907 while I was still at the home a group of young men of one of the churches in Wichita singled me out of the gang at the home and took me to the church. I believe it was Christmas Eve and fitted me out with clothes, shoes, cap, stockings, underwear, tie, a celluloid collar, a One-Dollar Ingersol watch, and a silver dollar. Also, along with the watch, I was given a nice watch chain. I still have the watch although it has not run in many years. The watches cost one dollar new and were always referred to as the One-Dollar Ingersol watches.

THE TOOKERS
1908

In late November 1908 I was sent to stay with some folks by the name of Tooker, who lived near Marion, Kansas. They had a boy of their own about seven years older by the name of Harold. Also an adopted baby girl named Hazel. Also a foster girl about fourteen or fifteen, who came from the same home I did. Her name was Lena Winfrey.

The Tookers lived on a farm six miles east of Marion.

I don't believe the officials from the home really investigated these people very closely. If they did they would not have sent Lena or I there. I really think the Tookers wanted us only for cheap labor.

Mr. Tooker believed in kids being kept busy. We always got up at four a.m. and we always had a bunch of cows to milk, hogs and horses to care for, besides the other regular daily chores. We seldom finished our days work until dark and then we would still have to milk cows, get in wood and water, feed and care for hogs, horses, etc.

The girl (Lena) worked just like a man. She helped plant crops, cultivated and harvested crops, milked cows, etc.

One winter day they all went to town and Mr. Tooker told me to clean out the barn. It had not been cleaned out for a long time and the manure was about fifteen inches deep. I worked hard all day and only had about half cleaned out when it was time to start the evening chores. It was after dark when they got home and I was busy with the chores. He went to put his team in the barn and he seen it was not all cleaned out. He asked me why the barn was not finished. I told him I had done the best I could. He called me a liar and proceeded to whip me with a buggy whip. Well, I made up my mind I would some day get even with him. I was only twelve years old and small for my age, but was doing a man's work with a team at the time.

I was always hungry. They would fix my plate of food with one piece of bread. I only got the one helping. They did Lena the same way.

I did get to go to school the first winter but we had all the chores to do before we left for school and after we came home at night. We walked about one and one half miles to school each way. At night I would fill two gunny sacks full of corncobs from where we fed the hogs. I would put four cobs in a can of kerosene for kindling to start the fire each morning. At about four a.m. Mr. Tooker would hit the floor with his boot and as I slept up in the attic (his boy slept up there with me). We had a ladder that went up there through the kitchen ceiling. I would awaken and grab my clothes under my arm and down the ladder I would come. I would start the fire in the living room and then in the kitchen. Get dressed and grab a lantern and head for the barn. He would not get out until after breakfast. Lena would soon join me with the milk buckets. We always milked from ten to twenty five cows. In the winter usually ten or twelve, in the summer as many as twenty-five. On Saturdays we would cut enough wood to last all week. On Sundays we would haul feed and stack it up for the stock all week. He had a patch of alfalfa growing next to the barn and feed rack. But when we harvested this hay he would always stack it on the far end of the field away from the barn. One day I asked Mr. Tooker why we did not stack this hay right by the barn in the feed rack? (There was plenty of room for it.) Then we wouldn't have to haul it across the field in the winter. That way all we would have had to do was fork it down to the stock. He told me that in as much as the way we were doing was good enough for his father it was good enough for him. He tried to live and work just like his parents before him. He had no thought of progress and seemed to me as if he always wanted to do everything the hard way.

About 1909 Mr. Tooker found out there was land to be had in New Mexico so he went out there and home-steaded 160 acres for ten cents an acre or sixteen dollars. There was a provision in the law that required the home-steader to establish residence on the land, build a habitable house on it and live there three months of the year so in March 1910 we moved out there. Mr. Tooker had sold his place in Marion area. I don't know if he owned the place outright or not. He had a sale and sold a lot of equipment, live stock, etc. Then he rented a railroad car. We loaded the car with four horses and two cows, farm implements, furniture, etc. He and I went with the car. Mrs. Tooker, Lena and the other children went out on the train. We went to Clayton, New Mexico. When we arrived there the family was awaiting us.

Mr. Tooker's homestead or claim as it was called in those days was about eighteen or twenty miles north of Clayton. At a place near what was called Dish Rag Cross-ing of the Currumpa Creek. Part of the Santa Fe Trail crossed the Currumpa there. It got its name it seems from an incident that was supposed to have happened there. There had been a cow camp there (The buildings were still there when we arrived.) Seems as two cowboys were living there and one day they had an argument and one of them was washing dishes and he hit the other in the face with a dish rag and he got shot for his efforts and killed.

At any rate Mr. Tooker's neighbor was a family by the name of McClary. The McClary's had moved out there from Marion. The McClary's had three boys, Wells, John, and Alfred. Also a daughter named Dora. The McClary's also had a nephew by the name of Edward Geer living with them. All the kids were teenagers from fourteen to eighteen. Geer was about seventeen.

The McClary's met us in Clayton with two wagons and teams so we assembled our outfit to move it on to the claim. It was customary in those days for neighbors to help each other so the McClary's were there to help us get settled.

There was a vacant one-room cabin on a place not far from the Tooker's claim and we settled in that until we could build a shelter for ourselves.

As soon as we got settled so we could get along we took all wagons and went to Clayton and got lumber to build with. We first built a boxcar type style of house with one large room and room in the end for the horses. Later they did a little better, but not much.

We finally got moved over there, but we had to haul all our domestic water about four miles and drive the stock to the creek about a mile and a half away.

Lena and I did most of the water hauling. We had a large barrel. We would put in the wagon. We put a canvas over the barrel and at the well. (A neighbor let us get water from his well.) He was a neighbor even if he did live four miles from us. I would pump the water in a bucket then carry it over and hand it up into the wagon to Lena.

48

She would pour it into the barrel. We would do this until the barrel was full.

Mr. Tooker bought twenty head of young cows right after we got there. Most of the time Harold would herd them out on the prairie, as we had no fences. We did build a small wire corral to hold the stock at night.

Mr. Tooker added on to his 160 acres by filing a desert claim on an adjoining piece of ground. The provisions on a desert claim was, it must adjoin the original homestead and the owner had to develop water on it by digging a well or building a storage pond, etc. Now he had a half section of land, 320 acres so he decided to fence it. Lena and I, when not doing any thing else, was put to digging postholes. They had to be twenty-four inches deep and a hole every rod (5 ½ yards). In other words the posts were a rod apart.

The year of 1910 was very busy year for all of us. Plowing new ground, planting it to Maize (Milo maize) and Kafir corn, also a garden and building fences, sheds, etc.

They finally drilled a well. It was 155 feet deep. We had to hand pump the water out of it, but that was better than hauling it. However we still drove the livestock to the creek for water.

Mr. McClary had a well drilled on his place. It was 176 feet deep. He also put in a hand pump. In setting the pump in place – I remember Mr. McClary was guiding the pump and the chain lifting it let go and the pump dropped about four feet. It caught both his hands under it and took off three of his fingers, Two on one hand and one on the other. Just below the knuckles,

We had a hard winter that winter of 1910-11, Lots of snow. I didn't get to school that year. We all slept in one large room. Harold and I slept in what was called a trundle bed. It was a bed with springs and mattress small enough to put on rollers and slide under the grownups bed.

I remember one night that fall I heard Mrs. Tooker ask Mr. Tooker about starting Lena, Harold and I in school. I heard him say Lena would probably marry some old boy and she didn't need any more schooling. I think she would have been in the seventh grade. As for me, he said I would probably never amount to anything and he saw no need of going to the expense of sending me to school.

New Mexico was a territory at that time and there was no laws protecting children's education rights. I made up my mind right then that if I never amounted to anything it would not be entirely up to him. I don't think he could have slapped me in the face and hurt me worse.

About that time I commenced to plan for the day when I would get away from him.

The next spring there was more plowing, fencing, planting, etc.

I remember he plowed a patch of ground and gave me a gallon bucket nearly full of popcorn to plant. I would use a hoe. I would make a gouge or small hole in the ground with the hoe drop three kernels of corn and cover them up. Take one step and repeat the performance. Well it takes a long time to plant a gallon of popcorn at three kernels at a time. I don't remember how long I worked at this, but almost two days, I am sure. I finally got tired of it and on the far end of the field there was a prairie dog hole and pushed it on down with the hoe handle. I still had nearly a half of the bucket left.

I went to the house and told them I had planted all the popcorn. However I didn't tell him I had planted part of it in a prairie dog hole. He told me if the corn came up more than three stalks to the hill I would get a licking. It never did.

One day I was talking with Ed Geer and I told him I was fed up with Tooker and planned to leave if and when I got a chance. He told me he would like to go along.

Incidentally Lena got away. Mr. Tooker got her a job in Clayton. (She was about 17 or 18.) He had planned to get her salary as I had heard him discussing it with Mrs. Tooker. However when he went to Clayton to get her first month's salary she was gone. The people who she was to work for said she had run away and got married. She was supposed to have married a farmer boy by the name of Grubb. Boy, was Tooker mad when he came home. I have never seen or heard of her since.

The Tookers were supposed to be quite religious. Every night before we went to bed they would read a passage from the bible and pray at mealtime. But he was not averse to taking anything laying loose from his neighbors. If there was ever a hypocrite he was one.

There was a thing they used to do that I have never seen anywhere else. After we would have supper we would wipe our plates clean with a piece of bread and then turn them over for the night. We would then eat off them the next morning at breakfast.

One day I met Ed Geer and I told him I was about ready to pull out. In the meantime Mr. McClary had gotten typhoid fever and died. Mrs. McClary ran the farm with her children. I don't know why Ed wanted to leave them. If he told me I don't seem to remember. I always thought the McClary's were nice people. I know they were hard working people. I do know that Ed always had good clothes to wear and I don't remember of ever seeing him going bare footed, like I did.

At any rate we set the leaving date on a Sunday in August 1911. It worked out just right. I usually had to herd the stock on Sunday so I told Ed where I would be that afternoon. I moved the stock to where I told him I would be and along late in the afternoon he met me. I was heading the stock on a pony. When he caught up with me we were about two miles from the house. He came up and said he was ready to go. I told him I was as ready as I would ever be. I got off the pony took his bridle off and hung it on the saddle horn and fastened it so it would not loosen and we took out. It was almost sundown by that time.

Now as I said Ed had a good suit of clothes, hat, good shoes, underwear, shirt, etc. All I had was a straw hat (farmers hat), blue work shirt and a pair of short knee pants. No shoes, socks, or underwear so we took out on foot.

We had no plans as to where we would go. Our guardian angel must have been watching over us and guiding us to where we ended up.

Note. As I said I was bare footed. Now, that New Mexico prairie has "pin cushion" cactus and in herding cows at times on foot I would step on them. They really hurt, but during this walk that night I did not step on one cactus. Some One was looking after me.

End Note

Elizabeth Bruckner (Dad's Mother) was born in Berlin, Germany on September 1, 1871. She married Louis Phillips (Dad's Father) on March 28, 1895 in St. Louis, MO.

Not much is known about Louis Phillips. He apparently lived in several locations near downtown St. Louis in the years from 1895 through 1901 but I had no success in finding out any more information on him. He passed away in 1901. There was a very large and terribly destructive fire In the St. Louis City Hall in 1900. Most of the vital records of birth, death marriages etc. were burned. This made it impossible to research the early years for many of the people from St. Louis. At that time no duplicate records were kept in the state capitol.

Dad was very hurt that his mother placed him in an orphan's home. We don't and will probably never know why she did this however I suspect it was possibly to save his life. Dad did tell me that old man Dauner would get drunk and come home and beat him. He never did say whether or not he would beat his mother but that was usually the case. One thing is certain, Dad never forgave his mother for placing him in the *home and he carried the hurt for the rest of his life. In fact she is never mentioned by name in the entire manuscript.*

Dad's sister Annie was born on January 18, 1904 and apparently Elizabeth was born a year later. I was not able to get a birth certificate for Elizabeth. Before Oklahoma became a state birth certificates were not always generated or filed. Annie's only existed since she must have needed it for other purposes and specially ordered it made up at a later date.

Dad's mother apparently was married to Michael Dauner as a mail order bride. There is also good evidence to believe that she came to this country in the same manner. Many young women immigrated to this country during these years under a mail order bride contract as that was one way to obtain the financing and the sponsorship needed to be allowed to enter the U.S.

I will relate one story that Dad told about his mother. One day a bum came to the door and asked for a meal. She said that she would feed him if he would chop some firewood. He said he would be happy to work for the meal but he was so weak from hunger would she feed him first. She agreed and allowed him to eat. When he finished he got up and started to walk away down the road. She said for him to come back and chop the firewood but he said goodbye and kept walking. She kept a 30-30-lever action rifle next to the kitchen door, which she very calmly raised and shot his hat off. He chopped the wood.

In telling about the drawing for property in Lawton Dad was exactly correct. On August 6, 1901 Michael Dauner drew Lot 11, Block 62 on the original Township of Lawton. Later on the address would list as 411 "E" Avenue. This must have been prime property since it was less than two blocks from the Courthouse. He paid $400 for the Lot. In 1909 he sold the lot to Ellen and John Crisp for $2500. I suppose that these were the parents of Bus Crisp that Dad mentions. At present a large downtown mall that stretches several blocks in all directions covers this property.

Heck Thomas did not die in the incident described. He passed away from natural causes some years later. This was not the only time that he was wounded in the line of duty.

Dad sort of glossed over the fact that orphans of the time were taken out of the home during the summer to work the farms but when cold weather came they were sent back to the home because the farmers did not want to feed them all winter. There is one record of his being placed with a CT and Alissa Docey of Rose Hill, Kansas on July 15, 1907 and re-turned to the Wichita house. There was no reason given for the return.

When Dad went to live with the Tookers in November of 1908 it precipitated radical changes in Dad's life. It is evident from the story that Dad hated Mr. Tooker and for good reason. It must be said in retrospect that Mr. Tooker probably did more in a left handed way to shape Dad's life in the future than any other single person.

First, when Mr. Tooker beat dad with a buggy whip it was not only brutal but it put the idea in to Dad's head to run away. Second, and more importantly, when Mr. Tooker said that Dad would never amount to anything and it was not worth the money to send him to school it fired up his determination to get as much education as possible and to run away from the Tookers. This event, more than any other, made him establish himself as a man in charge of his own affairs.

KENTON, OKLAHOMA SCHOOLS   1911-1912

Back Row, from left to right.

Ernest Allen, May Thornton, Meridith Hughes, "Ed Davidson, Florence Thompson, Cordia Cochran, S. Lynch, Emma Davidson, Lula Davidson, Lizzie Shannon, Helen Hubbard, Marion Chatterdon, Roselind Jones, Prof. "Wilson" "Howard Freeman, Oran Eddy,Nannie Derrick", Jimmie Allen, Merl Freeman, Rose Allen, Bill Wiggins, Guy Hubbard.

Bottom Row,

Templeton, Jim Dacy, Lawrence Johnson, Johnson, Floyd Hughes, Louise Dacy, Fred Kohler, Black Girl, Oran Templeton, Other Black Girl, Bob Thornton, Lillie Davidson, B. Thompson, Paul Jones, Nell Allen, Allen Thornton, Adel Thornton, Chas. Wiggins, Pansy Jones, Bert Allen, Marcia Malm, Mort Lynch, Edna Wiggins, Bethel Freeman, Elsie Kohler, Smokey Phillips, Doll Davis, Fidge Allen, Les Hughes, Walt Eddleman, Ralph Guy, Virgil Hughes, Burt Eddy.

Book Three

Cowboy

1911-1918

THE CIMARRON
1911 - 1918

When we started out we headed north. We crossed the Currumpa Creek. A little after dark we saw a light. It was late in the evening, as I said before when Ed met me. We went towards this light. It turned out to be a Mexican sheep camp.

One of them could talk very good English so he invited us to have something to eat. It turned out to be frijoles (Mexican beans) cooked with mutton with a pod of chili in it also tortillas and coffee. The frijoles were cooked in a big old cast iron Dutch oven over a campfire. They gave us a tin plate and cup. Boy, did we eat. I will never forget that meal. I have yet to eat a meal any better. We were both hungry. After eating we decided to go on. We thanked the Mexicans for the meal. They never asked any questions and we did not tell them what we were up to.

So we went on, we would walk a while. Then rest a while. Sometime before midnight the moon came up. After a while we could see daylight breaking. We did not see a house until way late. Then we came on a place and walked through the yard between the house and corrals. There was a dog there. He barked at us but didn't try to bother us.

About sunup we came to a homesteader's place. There was smoke coming out of his chimney. We stopped in and it was a bachelor. He gave us breakfast. I don't remember what he fed us, but we were hungry so I am sure we enjoyed it. After breakfast we thanked him and started on. Again I don't remember him asking any questions or what we may have told him.

After we left him it was only a short distance to the Clayton – Kenton freight road. When we reached that point I knew where we were. I had been there before. We were only about nine or ten miles from where we started.

At the time I had never heard of a place called Kenton so it meant nothing to either of us. But we followed the road all day. I don't remember where we got dinner. When we got thirsty we would go to some place off the road where cattle were watering. Usually there was a windmill with a stock tank.

Late in the evening we saw the roof of a house just over a small hill so we went over there and asked to spend the night. There were two ladies and some children there. They took us in and fed us and bedded us down for the night. The next morning they gave us breakfast. I don't remember if they asked any questions, but, being women, I imagine they did pump us. At any rate they were nice to us. We thanked them and went on our way.

I don't know where these women's men folk were, as in those days it was almost impossible to make a living on just the land and it was necessary for men folk to find employment elsewhere. It was nothing for men to be away from home for weeks at a time. Trying to establish a home on those plains at that time was hard. It meant lots of hard work and loneliness.

Along about noon or maybe a little after we saw a wagon coming towards us. When it got even we saw it was a lone man. He stopped us. We asked if he had water with him. He said yes and gave us his canteen. We got to talking and he told us to keep right on and we would come to a small town on the Oklahoma – New Mexico line, called Kenton. That was the first time we had ever heard of Kenton.

We learned this man's name was Eb Cochran. We also learned later there was a large Cochran family, several boys, some of whom I got acquainted with. However I never met any of the girls. Eb's father was a civil war veteran. Also the old man had served under Teddy Roosevelt in the Spanish-American War. There was also a boy (Bill) who also served in the Spanish-American War. (Both of their names are on the bronze plaque on the Buckey O'Neil statue in the Court House square in Prescott, Arizona. They both served with the first U.S. Volunteer Cavalry. (Rough Riders)

Eb was on his way to Clayton to see a dentist. He was having teeth trouble.

We went on our way and along in the afternoon we came to Kenton. August 15, 1911. We met a boy about my age, Charlie Wiggins, who told his father about us so Mr. Wiggins talked to us.

Before I go too far I should mention that Eb told us that when we arrived in Kenton we should look up a man by the name of Jack Potter and that Mr. Potter would see that we got a job of some kind.

The Wiggins ran a hotel in Kenton, in fact, the only one in town. They gave us our supper, let us stay the night and gave us breakfast the next morning. Of course all this after Mr. Wiggins had gotten our story. I don't think the story would have gone over so good except for me. I was the smallest and besides I was barefoot and with no clothes. (I was past fifteen and I only weighed 75 pounds and by reaching as high as I could I could barely reach six feet.) However Ed was much larger and taller, better dressed. I think that when they looked at me they took pity on me.

THE POTTER'S
1911

The next day after we arrived in Kenton, Mr. Potter came in from his ranch (He had a ranch west of town on the New Mexico line. The house was about two miles from town.) Mr. Wiggins told us he thought Mr. Potter would help us. He told us when you see a man bigger than any one you have ever seen that will be Jack Potter.

There was a store in town called the Hubbard and Potter Store. When Mr. Potter came in Mr. Wiggins said there is Mr. Potter now so Ed and I walked up to him. I looked up at him and said, "Are you Mr. Potter?" He said yes. I told him my name. Ed just stood there and did not say a word. First let me say Mr. Potter was the biggest man I had ever seen. I had to look straight up to look into his face. I said Mr. Potter can you give us a job? He looked at me and said, "I think I will call you Smokey", and he said to Ed, "I'll call you Sandy". (Ed's hair was sort of a sandy color.) He said I might be able to help you. Where are your clothes? I said I have them on – all I have. Well he said we will have to do something about that. Now he didn't ask where we came from or anything about us. He would never have asked our names.

That was and as far as I know still is one of the un-written laws of that country. Never ask any one were they came from or their name.

If you don't volunteer your name someone will hang one on you so Mr. Potter called me Smokey. More than sixty years have passed since that day and I am still known as Smokey in that area. There are people there who would not

Cornelia Potter, Dad and Col. Jack Potter
Clayton, New Mexico - 1948

know who you are speaking of should you mention Fred Phillips in their presence, but all knew Smokey.

Mr. Potter took me into the store and brought me underwear, shoes, socks, overalls, shirt and a three-dollar Stetson hat. One could get a pretty good hat for three dollars in 1911. He sent me back in a room, rather a storage room in the rear of the store, and told me to take off those farmer's clothes and throw them away, which I did. After dressing I came back into the store and he said you look a lot better. I saw some leather hatbands hanging behind the counter. He saw me looking at them and told the clerk to give me one of them, as no self-respecting cowboy would be without one. I believe I was as proud of that hatband than anything else he got me.

Now Kenton is in Oklahoma about a mile east of the New Mexico line and about six miles south of the Colorado line. It is in the Cimarron Valley on the Cimarron River. The altitude is about 4500 feet above sea level. There were cattle and alfalfa hay ranches all up and down the valley. The nearest railroad was Clayton, New Mexico about forty-five miles south. Now there is a railroad in Boise City, Oklahoma about thirty-five miles east of Kenton.

Mr. Potter took us out of doors and pointed up the river to the west and showed us a ranch house which was about two miles away, and told us to go up there and see Mrs. Potter and tell her he sent us up to work and to feed us and give us something to do.

When we got there we told Mrs. Potter what Mr. Potter told us. She gave us our lunch and asked us if we knew anything about working in a garden. Both of us being farmer boys it was what we knew best.

We worked in her garden the rest of the day. Her garden really needed working, as she could not get any of the cowboys on the ranch to do much in the garden. "A good cowboy deems it a disgrace to do anything that looks like farming." He will shy away from such things as garden tools or farming tools.

Mrs. Potter was a very small woman. She was probably about five feet tall and maybe she would weigh 110 to 115 pounds. Where Mr. Potter was extremely large. Well over six feet tall and I am sure he would weigh 250 pounds or more. Now Mrs. Potter didn't ask very many questions of us. She gave us our lunch and asked us if we could work her garden over. (In those days women and kids did the gardening.) We told her we could. I don't believe she was too happy with Mr. Potter picking us up and sending us to her.

We were right at home in the garden and we spent the entire afternoon cleaning it up, hoeing, etc. She was really pleased when she seen the job we did. After that when she wanted anything done she would ask for one of us.

The Potter family at home consisted besides Mr. and Mrs. Potter of one girl and two boys, Ethel about eighteen, Carl (or Jimmy) about 20 and Robert about 22.

There were several hands on the place. A man by the name of McNulty, Moose Eddelman, Eldon Crites and a youngster about sixteen years old by the name of Marvin Brown. (Called Scandalous John).

The next day Mr. Potter asked if we could drive a team or had ever worked in a hay field. We assured him we could take our place along side of any one in the hay field. And by time the day was over he was well satisfied we could.

Even if I was small he found out I could handle a team and do a good days work in the field. Ed Geer was much larger than I, but I could do as much work as he could.

The other hands did not hurrah us much. Especially after they found out we were able to do our part.

I will have to tell you about Scandalous John. He was the type who invited razzing. There are people like that; who believe anything someone tells them. He was like that so he was always being hurrahed and teased. He took everything serious.

There was a nice bunch of quail around the place. One day while we were resting after dinner (The Potter ranch always took two hours for dinner.) a bunch of quail came across the yard. Scandalous said where do these quail roost? (There is a large mesa just north of the ranch. In fact it forms a wall along the north edge of the valley. It is rather high and about half way up there is what is called a bench.) Along the valley floor at the foot of the mesa there are lots of what is known as buckhorn cactus. New quail usually hover on the ground under the cactus. I forgot to mention that at places on the bench of the mesa there were some scrub oak trees. When Scandalous asked where the quail roosted someone said they roosted in the oak on the bench. Well the bench on the side of the mesa was rather high and hard to climb. Bob and Mr. Potter all agreed that the quail roosted up there.

Early the next morning we heard old Scandalous crawling out of bed before daylight. He came in about breakfast time. We all saw him coming with a gunnysack in his hand. He came in and sat down to breakfast. He did not say a word. He did not have much to say all day, especially that morning. Finally during the noon break, someone asked him if he had any luck finding the quail roost? He said there are some of the darndest liars on this place I ever saw. He said there were no quail up there on the bench. Someone said, why? Didn't he find any quail? He said I was all over the bench this morning and there was no quail.

Just to show how gullible he was. Another stunt we pulled on him. A man by the name of Eddelman (Mose Eddelman's father) lived just down the river about a couple of miles (near Kenton). He had about one acre of watermelons. Mose would ride down there almost every evening after work and bring a couple home with him. One evening after work we saw Scandalous saddle up his pony and hang a sack on his saddle horn and ride out.

Now just below the house there was a bend in the river and in that bend was a sort of high bank, about six feet high. However there was a foot trail just above that led down to a rock ledge. Just under the ledge in the bend was a hole of water about ten feet deep. We used this place as a swimming hole.

Later we saw him come back and even if it was getting dark we could make out that he had something in the sack as he took it off of his horse. We saw him disappear under the riverbank. We knew he had raided Mr. Eddelman's watermelon patch so after he came to bed (we all slept in a bunkhouse) some of us crawled out of bed and went down there, jumped in and swam around until we found his melons. We brought them up and took them about a quarter of a mile down stream and sunk them again.

The next evening after work we saw Scandalous take off for the river. He was gone a long while. Finally he came back and we could see he was mad. We knew he had gone after a melon and he could not find them. He knew it was because some of us must have gotten them. Finally we slipped off and got them and brought them back to the rock ledge and ate them and left the rinds where Scandalous could find them. He really did not know who to blame so he blamed us all.

One day it was found out that the ladies were getting short on flour, as we were rather busy. Mr. Potter told Scandalous to get on his pony and ride into Kenton and get a fifty-pound sack, as it was only about two miles to town and back. Scandalous rode a small black Indian pony. He came riding in to the yard at a running pace. He had the sack of flour across the front of him, between him and the saddle horn. There was a fence across the back part of the yard. The horse must have been running away with him as he could not stop him and he did not stop until he was right at the fence. Well the horse stopped, but Scandalous did not. He flew right over that fence with the sack of flour. The sack burst. And you should have seen Scandalous. He was flour from one end to the other.

Mr. Potter was one of the old drovers who had helped trail cattle up from Texas to Dodge City and Abilene in the 1870's and early 1880's. He was never in too big of a hurry that he wouldn't take a two-hour noon siesta. He would always find a comfortable place where he could stretch out and take a nap. There was a long shed just west of the house. There was a pile of baled hay stacked up about six feet high. He got a tarp and spread it out on it. Then got a saddle blanket for a pillow. He would get up there and nap.

He always worked right along with us. We treated him as one of us. He would not have it any other way. Even if he was the boss you would never know it by his actions. Any one who did not know him would think he was one of the boys.

Now us young fellows did not need two hours rest at noon. One day some one said, let's have some fun with the old man. There was a pair of rope wire stretchers lying there.

We fastened them to an overhead beam on the shed. They tied a loop around Mr. Potter's feet and hoisted him up feet first. He was sleeping so sound he never knew we were roping him up until we had him almost up by the feet. Boy, did he squall, but he could take it and give it. We let him down and he just laughed about it.

There was never a dull moment at that place. Some of the boys had found a stray male goat and brought him to the ranch. That happened before we arrived as old Billy was a year or so old when I first met him. The boys had teased him until at times he could get mean, but he had his likes and dislikes. Some people he would not bother and then there were others he would fight.

He would come up and look one over. Smell of his leg and then maybe he would go on and start grazing and not pay any attention to you. Then again he might start backing up to a certain distance and then come running and knock one down. He would always hit his victims in the seat of the pants.

There was a man who was a friend of Mr. Potters by the name of Charley Rounds. He was a tall lanky fellow and very serious, always business. One day he rode in to see Mr. Potter. Mr. Potter happened to be out near the shed when Charley rode up. He got off his horse and walked over to Mr. Potter leaving his horse ground hitched a little way off. He and Mr. Potter were standing there talking when Billy came up and looked Charley over. I guess he did not like Charley. Charley did not pay any attention to Billy. Billy started backing up. Mr. Potter seen what old Billy was going to do so he eased around a little to put himself out of line. When Billy hit Charley in the rear end he rolled him. Billy stopped and looked Charley over them calmly turned and walked away. Charley got up; at first he could not figure what hit him until he got up and seen Billy looking at him.

Well it did not hurt Charley, but his dignity was rather shattered. He got on his horse and as he rode off he told Mr. Potter, "Jack, I will see you in town". After he left we all laughed. Mr. Potter never forgot.

We also had a big white goose. We called him Battling Nelson (At that time there was a middle weight fighter, who was really good called Battling Nelson). The goose was named for him. He would grab one by the pants leg and beat the devil out of you with his wing.

Before I forget I must tell this on Scandalous John. He liked to tell tall tales so he would be telling some of his big windy's and Mr. Potter would say, Scandalous are you sure you are not flowering that story off? Scandalous would say, not very much Mr. Potter. Not every much.

I have never seen Scandalous since. I heard indirectly he became a salesman for International Harvester Co., but this is only hearsay.

THE JONES'
1911 - 1912

I let it be known I was interested in going to school and as I mentioned before I let the Potters know that I would like to go to school and was willing to work for the chance.

So one day Mrs. Potter called me in the house and asked, "Smoky do you still want to go to school?" I told her yes. "All right" she said, "you go see Mr. and Mrs. Jones, who live in Kenton. I am sure they will give you the opportunity to go to school."

So I went to see the Jones as it was agreed I would get $5.00 a month and go to school, for which I would do the chores and help around the place.

The chores consisted of cutting and carrying in wood, carrying water from the well, feeding stock (usually a couple of horses and cows and calves), milking one or two cows feeding the chickens and cleaning the chicken house. I also had to help in the kitchen, (washing dishes, etc.)

Now Mr. and Mrs. Jones had seven children of their own. There were five girls and two boys. However of the two oldest I don't know who was the oldest. I believe it was Leona. I will say she was about 21, Albert was 20, Grace was 18, Roselind (Ted) was 15, Mary Ethel was 12, Pansy was 10, and Paul was 7. These numbers may not be their true ages, but it is close to it.

When I left the Potters, Mrs. Potter told me she thought I was doing the right thing by getting to school. When I left she kissed me on the cheek and said she would see me from time to time. I never forgot that kiss. (Almost forty years later when Mother, Bob and I were in Clayton we visited the Potters and when we left I kissed Mrs. Potter on the cheek. I told her I was returning what she gave me many years before.

Mr. Jones was also an old time cowboy. He also helped trail cattle from the lower Texas to Dodge City. He was one of the old time drovers.

He and Mr. Potter were partners at the time. They had leased a ranch near Boise City, Oklahoma, the old LKW outfit known as the LK's, I don't recall how many cattle they had over there.

Mr. Jones also had a ranch south west of Kenton in New Mexico on what was known as the Carrizozo.

Incidentally Eb Cochran (The man we met on the read on our way to Kenton) was taking care of Mr. Jones cattle and holdings on the Carrizozo).

School started in September and I entered the seventh grade. My teacher's name was Clay E. Wilson. I believe he was a graduate of the Oklahoma A and M College.

In October tragedy struck in the Jones' home. Their eldest son, Albert had been helping out over at the LK's. He came to town and met with some of his friends. He started to get on his horse to come home and some way his horse spooked or shied and threw Albert off striking his head on the only concrete walk in Kenton. (A short walk in front of the bank.) This walk was probably twenty feet long by about six feet wide. He died of a brain concussion. It was a sad day for the Jones. I did not know Albert very well as he was away from home most of the time, working at the ranch.

Mr. and Mrs. Jones were wonderful people. I often think of them, as they had seven children of their own and they still had room in their hearts and home for another waif. I often wonder if I was appreciative as I should have been for their kindness.

They treated me like on of their own. I had to do my part of the housework such as washing dishes, etc. Of course all of the outside chores were my responsibility.

I well remember they had the first car I had ever gotten very well acquainted with, a 1911 Ford Model T. After a while I got the idea I could drive it. One day Mr. Jones said, "Smokey do you think you can bring the car around to the side gate?" Like any youngster driving his first time I felt real proud of myself. I backed it out of the shed turned it around and headed for the side gate. It was sort of a downgrade and there was fence right in front of me. When I tried to stop along side the gate I couldn't so I ran right through the fence in front of me. Some how it came to a stop. Mr. Jones came over to look at the car. It was not hurt in the least. He started to laugh and said now you can fix the fence. Needless to say I never tried to drive that car again.

Well the winter of 1911-12 was a rough time for the Jones family. On February 21 we were having a box supper at the Kenton School. That evening while I was doing my chores it started snowing and by the time we were ready to go to the box supper it was really snowing hard. The schoolhouse was only about a fourth of a mile from the house. The road to town went right by the schoolhouse. The schoolhouse was on the edge of town. The road was only a sort of wagon road, cut down by horse hooves and wagon wheels and wore down about five inches.

So by the time we went to the schoolhouse the ruts were full of snow. We left the house about 7:30 p.m. It must have been about 10:30 when we started home and the snow was almost eighteen inches deep on the level by that time. We could barely see a light in one of the windows that Mrs. Jones very thoughtfully placed or we might have gotten lost. It was snowing so hard. Mr. Jones had gone out to the LK's the day before.

The next morning, Washington's Birthday, I went out to care for the stock. The wind had come up and was blowing and snowing so I could hardly breathe. We had a shed that was about forty feet long and probably twelve feet deep and open on the south end. The wind had blown the snow over the roof and drifted it almost as high as the roof. However there was a space between the drift and the back of the shed where there was no snow. One of the cows got down with her back down hill and feet up on the drift. She could not get up. I got a rope on her feet and turned her over. Then I helped her up and got her under the shed. The area between the shed and the stack was relatively clean of snow so I just opened the door and fastened it so it would not close and turned the stock into the stack yard.

All the time I was working I had to have a scarf over my nose and mouth in order to breathe.

I had to break the ice on the water tank so stock could get water. I also carried water and feed to the chickens. I got in water and lots of wood for the house. I put in most of the day out in the storm.

Mr. Jones had bought a new pair of Justin boots. Somehow he did not like them. (They cost $14.00 in those days). They were made to his measurements. He gave them to me. I was glad to have them during this storm.

When the storm was over we had about four feet of snow on the ground. Great drifts. There was a porch that covered the walk of the Wiggins Hotel, for the guests to use who had rooms on the second floor. This porch was about twelve feet from the ground. After the storm one could walk up the drift on to this porch.

The weather cleared up and the temperature dropped to 25 degrees below zero. Many cattle froze and starved to death. Cattle were found standing in drifts, frozen to death.

Mr. Jones and Mr. Potter lost heavily. In fact the storm broke them. They both were forced into bankruptcy, from which neither of them ever fully recovered.

When this storm hit the LK's did not have feed for their cattle. Prior to that time cattle were not fed. They lived on the native grass the year around and most years it was O.K. But when the ground was covered with four feet of snow they could not get to the grass.

There was a large outfit in Las Animas and Baca County Colorado, just north of us, called the Prairie Cattle Co. or as it was commonly known as J J was supposed to have 50,000 head that winter. They folded up.

I don't know how the homesteaders made out, but I was glad I was away from the Tookers.

All supplies for the valley had to be brought in by wagons from the railroad at Clayton. When the first wagon got thru there was only one fifty-pound sack of flour in Kenton, and other supplies were running low as well.

As I have said the Jones treated me as part of the family. I got the same considerations as their children. I had to go to Sunday school with theirs and at Christmas time I took part in school plays, etc. There was a Mrs. Eddy who always took charge of training kids for school or church plays. We all hated her. Boy, she was tough. Her husband, Mr. Eddy, was Mrs. Potter's brother. Their father was a doctor and was a civilian doctor for the army during the Spanish American War. They were working on the prevention and cure for yellow fever. He contracted the fever and died. I forgot to mention Mrs. Potter's Grandma Eddy lived with the Potters until her death. I have forgotten the date. She was a grand old lady. Also Mrs. Jones mother lived with them. Her name was Keyes.

She and her husband Calvin Keyes made several trips across the country from Independence, Kansas to California in 1849-50. The Keyes family settled for a time in the Walnut Grove area near Prescott, Arizona. They had a daughter (Sister to Mrs. Jones) born there in 1872.

The Jones men folks all met tragic deaths. Albert was killed by a horse. Mr. Jones was in Pueblo, Colorado and was killed by a streetcar. Paul was burned to death in a cabin fire in Clayton.

Leona married a man by the name of Jones and they lived in Albuquerque, N.M. Grace married a cowboy by the name of Paul Davis. I knew him well. Roseland married Wesley Labrier, an old school mate of hers and mine. They still live near Kenton and we had the honor of attending their fiftieth wedding anniversary on April 26, 1970. I don't know who Mary Ethel married. Pansy married a man by the name of Gardiner. They live near Apache Junction, Arizona.

As for the Jones' grandchildren, I only know what Roseland and I were near the same age and we got along fine unless we got to arguing about washing dishes.

Getting back to Eb Cochran, he always got out of bed at four a.m. He would build a fire, get breakfast, then sit around and wait for the daylight. I could never understand why however he always was in bed by eight o'clock in the evening.

One time I think it must have been during Easter Vacation, Mr. Jones sent me up to the Carrizozo camp with Eb. He also hired an old man by the name of Johnny Mair, a civil war veteran. We were to help Eb put up a windmill tower. Mr. Mair considered himself somewhat of a carpenter.

I had to sleep with the old man. Mr. Mair must have been in his late sixty's and was more of less crabby while I was young and full of pep.

One night I woke up and the old man was hitting me in the back and every time I moved he would hit me and tell me to be quiet I got so I just curled up on the edge of the bed and stayed there.

As for early risers, that seemed to be characteristic at the time, especially among farmers. While staying at the Tookers we always got up at four a.m. except Sundays, when we arose at five a.m. I remember lots of times when I would say I'd be glad when Sunday comes so I can sleep until five a.m.

THE RECORDS
1912 - 1913

I left the Jones the next June after school was out. I got a job working for a Dr. Regnier near the edge of Colorado. I got $10.00 a month and board.

He had a small ranch and lived with his daughter, an old maid. Her name was Carrie. Dr. Regnier had arthritis awfully bad and could not get around very good. They also had a small Post Office called Regnier. I was only there a short time.

The Dr. liked wine and he bought a fifty-gallon barrel. He had a cellar in the hill in the rear of his house. Every time I got a chance I would tap the barrel. I don't know if he ever caught on or not.

As I said, they had a small Post Office and the mail came from the railroad to Kenton. Then relayed by horseback to Regnier. Both the mail from Kenton to Regnier and from Regnier to Carrizo was carried three times a week, Tuesday, Thursday and Saturday.

Ed Geer got the job of carrying the mail from Kenton to Regnier. He was working for another man I don't remember his name. A man by the name of Vesta Bray had the contract carrying the mail from Regnier to Carrizo.

One day Mr. Bray asked me if I would like to come to work for him. He would pay me $2.50 a month more or $12.50. I was getting $10.00 a month from Dr. Regnier. The $2.50 looked good to me so I told the Dr. what Mr. Bray had offered me. He asked if I was going to take it? I said yes unless he would match it. I guess it made him a little mad; so he said OK take it.

I went to work for Bray. He lived in a side canyon on the upper Carrizo Creek. I carried the mail the rest of the summer for him. After I got adjusted he and his family (He had a wife and a little daughter) took off for about three weeks and left me alone. That is when I had to learn to cook or starve.

He smoked cigarettes and he always bought his Bull Durham and cigarette papers in quantity lots so while he was gone I got to fooling around with his tobacco and started to smoke.

I commenced to inquire around for another chance to go to school.

I had saved my money and gathered a few clothes. I finally heard from a man by the name of Record. John Record lived about a mile west of Kenton. It was arranged that I would stay there and work for my board and go to school. It was not much for my work, but I felt it was worth it to have a chance to go back to school. This would be my eighth grade year, and I was sixteen years old.

After leaving Tooker and getting to stay at these homes where I got all I wanted to eat I commenced to fill out and grow.

I told Mr. Bray I had a chance to go to school. He did not like me leaving him. However he did say he thought I was doing the right thing.

So in the fall of 1912 I started back to school. My teacher was a man by the name of Long. I don't know where he came from, but we got along with him OK, however he was not as strict as he should have been.

The Record family consisted of Mr. Record and his wife, Emma, who was at least twenty years younger than he. They had several children, all rather young. I don't remember any of their names.

There was a lot of things Mrs. Record would rather do than keep house, so I was kept busy both inside and out.

Mr. Record was away from home some, as he would occasionally do some hauling for ranches between Clayton and the valley. It took four days for a round trip. I would have to care for the stock as well as the regular chores. Also help in the house, garden, etc. In other words Mrs. Record was of the type who did not believe in doing today that which could be put off until tomorrow. She was just plain damn lazy. She would let the dirty clothes pile up for as long as she could until finally we had no clean clothes to wear. Then Mr. Record and I would have to help her.

One day he and I was out after wood and we was in Charlie Potter's (Mr. Potter's nephew) pasture. Mr. Record and I had a nice load of wood on the wagon and were starting home. When he said, "Look Smokey, there is a calf laying under that cedar tree. I believe he is lost." (Now anyone who knows that when a cow had to go along way to water and she has a young calf she will hide the calf where she thinks it will be safe, go to water and come right back to her calf.) Mr. Record said "Lets take him home. He might die there." He stole that calf. We took that calf home. We had a cow there with a young calf, so we put this calf with his cow and she raised them both.

I went on to school all winter. I got into trouble one time that winter. We older kids in the sixth, seventh and eighth grades were moved to an older building that had been a school. We did not have enough desks so some of us used tables and drop leaf desks.

One of the Eddy boys, Oren (we called him John Brown) sat between where I sat and the entrance. I sat at a table in the far corner. We were coming in after our noon recess one day and as I came in I leap-frogged over John Brown's desk and landed in my chair. I hardly hit the chair until Mr. Long back handed me, and knocked me clear out on the floor. All of us kids had been more or less tormenting him and I guess he was getting pretty well tired of it.

Another time a boy by the name of Ernest Allen, we called him Hickory, got some long fire crackers about four inches long and three-fourths inch in diameter. He gave me one. It was spring and the days were getting warm. We had a wood stove in the middle of the room. We were allowed to put all our waste paper in the stove and then burn it. I rolled up this firecracker in some paper and took it to the stove. As I passed Hickory's desk I gave him a nod. I put my paper in the stove and as soon as I sat down he got up and did the same thing only he lit the paper. Pretty soon the firecrackers went off. They blew the lids and doors off the stove. The stovepipe came down and the kids went out of there a flying. You might guess what a turmoil that created. Mr. Long did not do a thing about that. Both of us, Hickory and I thought sure we would get a licking for that. It was after that he knocked my out of my chair. I really don't blame him. He should have whaled the hell out of both of us right then. We had it coming.

While I am on that subject, in those days kids were just as lively and mischievous as they are today, but we were controlled. We knew what to expect if we got out of line. A teacher knew he had permission of the parents to chastise a youngster if he deemed it necessary and most times if a kid got whaled at school he could expect to get another at home. Also if a youngster got smart or out of line anywhere the first adult who came along would straighten him out.

I remember while still at home there was a man who used to visit our house and he used to play with me at times. One day I met him on the street and walked up behind him and slapped him on the rear and said, "Hi there Hesse." His name was Hesse. He turned and slapped me up side the head and knocked me rolling. My mother happened to see it and when I got home I got another for being too familiar with my elders.

We had no juvenile delinquency as such, not like we have today. We were taught respect for authority. When we were told to do or not to do something we knew better than to question the order. When we spoke to an adult we said, "yes sir" and "no sir", "yes madam" and "no madam".

Getting back to the Records. I remember one day Mrs. Record told me to got into Kenton for something. I forgot what it was. At any rate she gave me some eggs to take in to pay for her purchase. We put them in a milk bucket. There must have been four or five dozens in the bucket. I saddled my pony, got on him and the bucket hanging on my arm. It had snowed some the night before. I had to go through Ed Fouleman's Mom's yard. I had to cross an irrigation ditch. There was a slight raise on this crossing and I was riding at a slow lope or gallop. After crossing the culvert over the ditch and starting down the other side my horse's feet slid out from under him and down we went. I fell on the egg bucket mashing it flat and breaking every egg. All I could do was get the horse up and go back to the house and get more eggs. We had lots of them as they had lots of chickens. Boy was Mrs. Record mad. Mr. Record laughed when I told him what happened and eggs were valuable those days. (Ten cents a dozen.) This was the year of 1912-1913.

I worked for Mr. Record for a while just before and after school was out. I was needing money however especially for clothes. He had some irrigation ditch work that needed doing and he and I agreed that I would get $15.00 a month working for him. This was in the first part of April. School was out the middle of May. He went good for the clothes I needed so I sort of stocked up. I stayed until about the middle of June 1913 when I quit him. At the time he owed me about $40.00. It took me over three years to get all the money.

The hay ranchers were starting to put up alfalfa hay. At the time alfalfa seed was the real paying crop along with cattle. I went to work in the hay fields the rest of the summer and fall. I had a school buddy by the name of Allen Thornton. I used to visit at their home a lot. He and I worked the hay fields together. We got $1.50 a day and board, which was the going wage at the time.

Allen and I was helping a preacher by the name of Guy put up hay that late summer when Allen's Uncle Bob Davidson, who had a hay ranch nearby came over and asked him and I if we would help put up the Davidson's hay. I was in another part of the field when Mr. Davidson asked Allen. Allen spoke for me and said we would. We still had a couple of days work for Guy. That evening Allen and I decided to go into Kenton. Which was not very far. On our way to town we passed through Davidson's hay field. When we saw that field we decided we did not want any of that. It was nearly all sand burr hay. To any of you who don't know what sand burrs are, they are a very sharp seed on the hay. They get all over you and hang on, very irritating, and when they hang on your hide and when you pull them off they nearly always draw blood. I told Allen I did not believe I wanted any of that. He said he did not either so we went over to Davidson's after we finished Guy's and stayed the night.

The next morning we hit the floor at four a.m. However Allen and I had talked it over during the evening before and said we wanted none of the sand burr hay. When we went to breakfast all we had was biscuits, water gravy, fried salt pork and coffee. This breakfast alone was enough to cause us not to want to work for Mr. Davidson. We told him we did not think we would help him. We thought we would go up into Colorado. Now Mr. Davidson did not like that one bit. He never spoke to me after that.

Getting back to that breakfast we were spoiled. Everywhere we had been working we were fed real good. Usually we could expect ham or bacon and eggs, steaks, buckwheat cakes, hot biscuits, the works. I have seen the time since when I could call the Davidson breakfast a banquet.

We did go up into Colorado. Allen's folks lived up there. But I got a job working for a Mr. Shannon in his apple orchard. He had about fifteen acres of orchard so we picked apples, made cider, etc. While there I received word that my mother had died. When I was still at Tooker's I had written my mother, but never heard from her so one day Mr. Tooker told me it was foolish to write as he had heard she was dead. When I heard she had died she had been dead about a month. I still don't know how the letter caught up with me in the fall of 1913, unless Mr. Dauner had written the home, and they forwarded the letter to Tooker. He in turn sent it to me. They knew I was in Kenton because I had written and asked them to send me a few articles I still had there. Among them was the watch I mentioned before. Getting word of mother's death that late I decided not to go to Lawton.

After I got out of work that fall I went up river and put up at Potter's ranch. They had sold the ranch near Kenton and had another about eight miles further up the river. As was the custom those days about every ranch hand had a place he called home when out of work. I always had a welcome at their place when out of work or between jobs. I could always go there. Of course I was expected to pull my weight. Do enough around the place to pay for my keep. I did chores, fixed fences, hauled wood, helped clean irrigation ditches, feed cattle, etc. That was known in those days as riding chuck line. Food was called chuck.

There was an old man in the country by the name of Tyne Arnold. Old Tyne would never work in the winter. That is he would never commit himself to a steady job where he had to get out every day. He would ride the chuck line all winter. He would stop at some ranch and would hang around, do chores, help around for his keep. He would stay until some one made him mad then he would saddle his pony, tie his war bag on him and leave without saying a thing. He would then go somewhere else and do the same thing. Maybe before spring he would come riding in, put his horse in the corral, throw his war bag in the bunkhouse and make himself at home. Billy Stewart reminded me of him. He was about Billy's size and age. He was also an old bachelor. I asked him one time, "Tyne why did you never get married?" He said, "Well Smokey, it's like this, I never thought I could sleep all night with a woman and eat her cooking the next morning."

We had another old-timer there who would not work in the winter. Only he saved his money in the summer. About the first of November he would move into some empty line camp and live alone all winter. He had a good camp bed and few cooking utensils, coffee pot and Dutch oven. His name was Thompson. I don't remember his first name if I ever heard it. All I knew him was by the name of Sugar Lip. I believe Mr. Potter hung that handle on him.

The next spring in 1914 after I had spent the greater part of the winter at the Potter ranch, Mr. Potter asked me to stay on and offered me $20.00 a month so I agreed. At the time we were more or less camping at this place. There was Mr. Potter, his son Robert, a nephew, who's name was Espy. We called him Doc.

Note on Mrs. Record,
There was a merchant by the name of Benny Clements in Kenton. He ran a sort of notion store, candy, tobacco, fruits, vegetables, etc. His place was sort of a loafing place especially in the winter. He always had a nice warm fire and there were chairs around the stove. His front door was one of the few in town that had glass almost its entire length.

One day some of us were in Benny's (as we called his place). When Mrs. Record came in, it was cold and windy out side. The door opened in as usual so when she came in she turned her back on it to close it. Well she pushed her rear end right through the glass. Old Benny looked up and said, "You sure played hell".

That glass would not be replaced in Kenton. I doubt if he got a replacement in Clayton. I don't know the location where he got it. At any rate I do know the Records had to pay for it, because knowing Benny like we did he would never take that loss. And it would not surprise me that if the truth was known he padded the real bill.

Benny was another bachelor. As I intimated, Benny Clements was very frugal, and we all knew it. He was very religious in his way and a strong Baptist. He always went to church Sunday night, and always on Wednesday night. One evening some other fellows and myself was sitting on the edge of the sidewalk in front of Benny's store. There was a window there and inside we could see buckets of candy. We were sure it was candy. There were loose lids on the buckets. Someone said I wonder if that window is locked so we tried it and it wasn't. We pushed it up far enough so we could

93

reach in and remove these lids and help ourselves to the candy. We ate all we wanted, closed the window after putting the lids back. This happened on one of Benny's church nights. We tried the window again the next time Benny was gone, but the window was well locked.

THE POTTER'S
1914 - 1915

As I said Mr. Potter, Robert, Doc and I batched or camped at this place.

Mrs. Potter and Grandma Eddy lived in town. Mr. Potter would go in about once a week.

We were busy cleaning irrigation ditches in the early spring. Irrigating alfalfa, when we had water. We had lots of fun there. As I said before there were no dull moments around that old man. We called him old man. However I don't think he was over 45 when I first met him in 1911.

He was a person who enjoyed life and he liked to have young people around. He would play tricks on anyone for a laugh. Also if anyone tricked him he could laugh at himself.

One time in early spring, I'll say possibly it was in April. It had rained a good rain and the river had run quite a bit. We thought we had better take a ride up to the dam and check the ditch. It was about four miles up there. On our way back we came to a place were we had to cross a wash. The water was running a nice stream in it. Right below the trail was an out-cropping of rock or ledge. Over the years rain water running over this ledge had washed a rather large hole, possibly 50 feet long, 8 or 10 feet wide and about 4 feet deep where the water ran over this rock and dropped off into this hole. The water was nice and clear. Just about the time we got across Mr. Potter said I am thirsty lets get a drink. I said OK so we climbed off our horses. He knelt and bellied down and drank right at the edge were the water ran over the rock. When he finished I did the same. As I was drinking he put his foot in my rear end and pushed me over into the water hole. I went in as if I had dove, completely under. Boy, that water was cold and we were at least two miles from home. I almost froze before we got home. He never really laughed very loud. He had sort of a chuckle. When he was amused. I told him I would get even.

Another time he pulled one of his tricks, it was summer and we were putting up hay. We had taken the box off of the wagon and put a hayrack on in its place so we just put the wagon box on the ground. The main irrigation ditch was above or up hill from where we put the wagon box.

We had an old timer there by the name of Nicholson. He was at least in his 60's. He was sort of a cantankerous old fellow. As it was nice warn summer weather most of us slept out of doors. Also there was not room enough in the house for all of us.

Mr. Nicholson put a lot of hay in the box and made his bed on the hay. It so happened that the open end of the box was just right for what Mr. Potter had in mind. He very seldom went to bed very early. He liked to tinker around when the nights were warm, especially on moonlit nights. We all went to bed and did not pay any attention to him. However all this time he was making a small trench from the ditch to the end of the wagon box where Mr. Nicholson was sleeping. The ditch was running full at the time. When he got everything set just right he opened the ditch and turned a large stream of water into the box. It did not take long for Mr. Nicholson to realize he was laying in water. He came out of there as mad as a hornet. The next morning he left us. I don't know how he got through the rest of the night, because his bed was soaked.

About that time there seemed to be a lot of bums in the country. Although we were approximately 50 miles from any railroad, we had a couple come to our camp.

In the cabin where we ate and slept, we had a "round up" chuck box fastened to the wall and when the door was opened it made a cook table. This chuck box we used as a cupboard for cook's supplies and it was in the corner. Just across in the opposite corner was the cook stove. We had no bedsteads. We only had rolled up camp beds. In daytime we used them to sit on. At night we rolled them out on the floor to sleep. Starting on the far end was Mr. Potter's bed, then Robert's, Doc's and then me. There was a little area between where I rolled my bed and the stove.

On this particular evening when we got in it was about dark. We took care of our team and then went in to eat. There was a stranger there. While we were eating I noticed there was something about the way he was acting. He watched every move I made. I also noticed there was some chain lying on the floor under the cook's table. I knew this chain belonged out of doors. Knowing Mr. Potter and Bob like I did I suspected that there was something going on. After eating I went outside. Bob followed me and told me the old man had intimated to this stranger that I had been bitten by a skunk and was subject to spells, especially during the phase of the full moon. There was a bright moon that night. When I had one of these spells I had to be chained up, because I became violent. When we went to bed that night we put the stranger between the stove and me.

The next morning when we got up, we noticed the stranger had a large stick of stove wood right along side his bed where he could get his hand on it. I imagine had I even groaned very loud that night he would have worked me over.

As I mentioned before I had told Mr. Potter that I would get even for dunking me One day I got my chance. The main ditch had been running good and all at once it stopped. The ditch ran dry at the house. Mr. Potter and I hitched the team to the wagon and went to find out. Sure enough about a couple of miles above the house we found the border on the down hill side washed out. We found a large cottonwood log nearby so we hitched the team on it and put it across the break in the border. There were a lot of boulders around there so we carried some of them and threw them in front of the log. We had to walk out on the log to put them in place.

I got to thinking how funny it would be to dump the old man in the ditch. On one end of the log there was a short limb stuck up. We had the break almost fixed so as Mr. Potter carried the last rock out there I waited until he dropped it and then I took hold of the limb and rocked the log. By that time the ditch was running almost full and there was about 2 and a half feet of water there. Mr. Potter's footing was precarious anyway and when I rocked the log he went off of there into the water. When he hit he went WOOF. He went out of sight and came up sputtering. He crawled out on the upper side on his hands and knees. Then he realized I was the cause of it all as I was standing there laughing. His face got real white and he looked straight at me. For a second or two I know he was mad enough at me to kill me. All at once he started to grin and he remembered what he had did to me. Besides this was a real warm day. He started to chuckle and said, "I guess we had better go home".

Since then I have thought many times of what could have happened. We had been putting those large rocks there in front of that log and as large and heavy as he was he could have very well broken his back and could not have been able to crawl out of there. As big as he was I would had a rough

98

time getting him out. He might very well have drowned. I would never pull a stunt like that again.

That fall Mr. Potter decided we should have better quarters for the winter so he decided we would build a half dugout. We dug down in the ground about three and half feet by sixteen feet wide by twenty feet long. We laid rock walls up from the bottom about seven feet high. That made the walls about three and a half feet below ground level which made the walls about seven feet and eighteen inches thick. We put a window on the east, a door on the south, a large fireplace on the north end and finished it by putting in a concrete floor.

After it was finished we lived and slept there and cooked and ate in the cabin. It was really comfortable. In winter we would get some large piñon logs for the fireplace.

There was a half Mexican who lived in the area by the name of Lee Henley and he was good at rockwork and fire-places so he worked with us.

Oh yes, the roof was supported by cottonwood logs, then cedar limbs, brush and finally about a foot of soil.

The spring and summer of 1915 I worked at different jobs. One day I seen Mr. Potter and he told me he had gotten the contract to carry the mail from Kenton to Regnier and asked me to do it. I was to get $20.00 a month and board. I would stay at a man's place on the Gallinas (pronounced Guy een us). The name was Bill Hughes. Bill Hughes family consisted of his wife and two daughters. They were small and I have forgotten their first names.

I carried the mail three times a week, Tuesday, Thursday and Saturday. I only did that about three months until Mr. Potter sold the contract.

I will take time out to explain this mail delivery deal.

The routes between Kenton - Regnier, Regnier – Carrizo were called star routes. Proposals were sent out every four years asking for bidders to deliver mail to these places three times a week.

If I remember right, Mr. Bray took the contract to deliver mail from Regnier to Carrizo for $400.00 a year. I don't know what Mr. Potter was getting a year.

After I lost the mail-carrying job I saw a man by the name of Wagner in town one day and he said, "Smokey what are you doing these days?" I told him I was between jobs. He asked me if I would help him deliver some cattle to the railroad at Des Moines, New Mexico. I told him I would.

Wagner's real name was Bob, but everyone called him Charlie. His family consisted of his wife, three daughters and a son. I don't remember the girl's names. The boy was called Robert Jr.

Now Charlie Wagner was another cantankerous old boy. He had been ear marked. The story around the country was that he had been caught stealing cattle and some cowboys earmarked him by cutting off the top of each ear.

I believe it was in late October or early November of 1915 we took the cattle about 200 head of cows and a few old bulls to the railroad. We pushed them into the stockyards in Des Moines late on the afternoon of the sixth day out from the ranch they were supposed to be loaded on cars and shipped to Denver. However, there were no cars available for loading the next day. The next day Charlie told me to move them out on the prairie at the foot of the Sierra Grande Mountain and let them graze so we moved them out. Now he said, "I'll send some one out to relieve you at noon." I forgot to say there were six to seven of us on the drive.

The only name I can remember of the gang was Walt Smiley besides Charlie himself.

At any rate it was a miserable day. I recall it tried to snow, sleet, rain then the sun would come out, then it would cloud up and start all over again.

Well noon came and no relief. In fact no one came to relieve me all day. Now I want it made plain here, in those days if a person were placed in the position I was he would not leave his herd no matter what the cause. It never entered my mind that I should leave the cattle and go look for my relief, however I understood we would pen them in the railroad stockyard again that night. When it commenced to get late I did push them into the stockyards. I seen there was plenty of water for them. As it was only a short distance into town, I fed and watered my horse, then went to town.

I started looking for Charlie. I found him on the street talking to someone he knew. I said, "Where are the other fellows?" He said, "Where have you been all day." I said, "I was with the herd." He said, "Oh my God, I forgot to send you a relief. I know you had no dinner, come on and get some supper." He took me to a café to eat. When we found the other guys they were all pretty well liquored up.

The next day we loaded these cattle. I think Walt Smiley went to Denver with them. After the cattle were disposed of we loaded the wagons (we had two with us) with supplies for the ranch and headed home. We only made about five miles that evening before dark so we made camp. That night it snowed. There was a nester (settler) who had just completed a big barn. He let us move into that for the night. The next day it snowed and blew all day so we just stayed there that day. By driving late we got back to the Wagner ranch the third day. Mr. Wagner only hired me for one job so I went back to Potters.

Now as I said Charlie Wagner was quite a character. He could never keep any hand very long. He was cranky; also if he saw any of his hands look at one of his daughters twice he would find an excuse to let him go. His girls all had to elope to get married.

One day after I finished with Wagner. I had a call from Eddelman. He lived near Kenton. He owned one of the few power hay balers in the country. He said he had a contract to bale a lot of hay for a man by the name of Sam Collins in Colorado. He asked if I would go along so I said OK. We, Mr. Eddelman, his son Rich, a fellow called Bud Carter took a tent and camp outfit and went up there. It took us two days to take the outfit to Collins ranch. We worked pretty hard, but we had a good time too. We had quite a bit of snow, but it did not bother us as the hay was stacked and all we had to do was push the snow off and go on baling.

There were lots of quail around there. Mr. Collins loaned us a quail trap and we ate plenty of quail. Someone has said one could not eat a quail a day for thirty days. I don't remember if we tried it, but we ate a lot of them. And I don't remember getting tired of them.

After finishing Mr. Collins baling we moved back to Kenton. About the time we got the outfit back Mr. Eddelman said, "I have a contract to bale for Alex McKenzie". Alex McKenzie was a Scotsman and a sheep man. He also had lots of hay. His sheep were over in Colorado about thirty miles from his home ranch. He had to haul this hay to his sheep so that is why he wanted it baled. His hay ranch was about twelve miles up river from Kenton.

Bud Carter quit us and joined the Army so we got a brother of Eb Cochran to help us. He was older than Eb. His name was George. George was married and had a family of his own. I don't remember how many boys or how many girls. I do remember one of his boys, and I will mention him later.

We spent a couple of weeks at McKenzie's. He had a house for us to live in however we did our own cooking.

He needed men to do ditch work, clean our irrigation ditches. Now we did this work with horses and scrapers, not pick and shovels. There was another old boy there that I knew well, Jim Smiley, the brother of Walt's.

Now Jim Wiggins was another of the old timers, who did not care how long one slept in the morning as long as he was up at 4:00 a.m. and as this happened to be in the middle of winter it was always long before daylight. We never ate supper until away after dark however I will say he always fed good. In fact, I don't remember anyone in that country that did not feed good unless it was the Davidson's (Afore mentioned).

After we had been at the Wiggins ranch a few days Jim Smiley commenced to complain about the long hours. I did not say much, but I was also getting fed up. One night we were at supper and Jim Smiley said to Jim Wiggins, "Mr. Wiggins, I believe I will take off tomorrow. I want to go into town. I have some business to care for." Mr. Wiggins said, "It happens I am going to town tomorrow maybe I can take care of your business for you." Smiley said, "I don't think so". Mr. Wiggins said, "Tell me, maybe I can." Smiley said, "I will tell you. I want to trade my bed off for a lantern." One has no use for a bed around here." Mr. Wiggins said, "O.K., but you won't need to come back. I spoke up and said to Smiley. I guess I will go with you. There was several of those Wiggins.

In those days we all had our own beds and took our bed everywhere we worked. Usually a tarp and a few blankets.

There were Jim, Tom, Charlie and Jack. Charlie was the one who owned the Wiggins Hotel, where I spent my first night in Kenton.

Tom had a little ranch nearby. Speaking of Tom, I met him early one morning in the Eklund saloon in Clayton. He was sitting there on a chair, his elbows on his knees, chin in his hands. I patted him on the shoulder and said, "Tom, what are you thinking about?" He said, "Hello Smokey, I was sitting here thinking about those two son-in-laws of mine. You know one could rake Hell over with a fine-tooth comb and could not find two ornerier s.o.b.'s.

Tom only had two daughters, no boys. One married a fellow by the name of Dick Young. I did not know him. The other married a fellow by the name of Cal Carter, brother of Bud's.

Jack Wiggins was another like Billy Stewart. Small wiry, but he was a lot uglier. He had one eye out and could be mean. He always carried a big six shooter, which he called his equalizer. He would be drinking and he would always get in an argument when drinking. He would pat his gun and say, "This makes me as big as any man." Old Jack never married.

In those days, Oklahoma was dry, but just across the line in New Mexico and Colorado was wet. Most of the time when the boys wanted to get together and enjoy themselves they would send to Clayton and get that old $1.00 a gallon jug whiskey.

One time a gang of the boys was in town and somebody brought in some whiskey for them and they were all having a good time. They went into Shannon's Drug Store and found out he had some roman candles left over from the 4th of July. They bought them all and got out in the street and started shooting them. Pretty soon they started shooting at each other. One of those balls of fire went right by Jack's face on his blind side. Really too close for comfort. I don't think it hit him in the face, because if it had hit him it might have burned him. At any rate he said what the Hell are you trying to do and he pulled that old hog leg out of his pants and started shooting it down the street. You should of seen that gang get around the corners of buildings.

When that gang could not get whiskey, especially Jack Wiggins and some of his cronies would drink Peruna, a laxative they used to sell in the drug stores. It was made of Prune juice, alcohol, etc.

Kenton is almost a ghost town now however I have seen it when it was pretty lively.

What Tom Wiggins said about his sons-in-law was not far from wrong. As I said I did not know Dick Young, but I did know Cal Carter. His wife Bertie went to school with the rest of us kids. Cal never did a good days work in his life. He usually could be found in a poker game if there was one available. I never knew Cal Carter to do any work.

Cal was quite a gambler. There were several fellows in the country like that. They never had a job. But always had good clothes and money in their pockets.

There is an old saying that there is about 10 cents difference in the man who works, and the man who don't and the man who don't work had the dime.

One time a stranger came to town. Some of the boys, Cal was one of them, got the stranger in a game. Seems as, in one hand the ante was short. I believe they were playing nickel ante. Cal accused the stranger of not anteing. It wound up by Cal calling the stranger a liar. Whereby the stranger whipped out a knife and cut Cal's throat, just missing his jugular vein on both sides. It did not kill him, but the last time I saw him, he had that scar across his throat.

In 1950 Mother, Bob and I was on a trip. We were going to Detroit to visit Kathleen and Paul. We went by way of Clayton. We saw both Mr. and Mrs. Potter. They were getting old. Both passed 80 years. Mr. Potter had to wear a hearing aid. But was still his jovial self. He had served as state representative from Union County, and was at this time justice of the peace in Clayton. He married a Mexican couple that morning right out on the front porch of his house.

He had been doing some writing about his adventures as a drover on the Dodge City drives. He also wrote a sort of autobiography in which I am mentioned.

THE HUBBARD'S
1916 - 1917

One day I got word that George Hubbard wanted to see me. This was about the first of March 1916 so I looked him up. He asked me to go to work for him steady at $25.00 a month so I agreed and about the middle of March I went there.

The Hubbard family consisted of Mrs. Hubbard, a son Guy, and a daughter Helen, also George's mother, Grandmother Hubbard. Helen was the oldest of the Hubbard children. I had gone to school two years with both of these kids.

The Hubbard's had the old Potter ranch where I went when I first went to Kenton and the Cimarron. He raised lots of alfalfa hay also had quite a few cattle.

Now when I say I worked for George Hubbard. I can say it without reservations. I really worked. I hit the floor about 5:00 a.m., but we always tried to be in by dark. But between 5:00 a.m. and dark we put in a days work.

Now George did not like to work. I don't believe I have ever seen him do a days work, but he wanted every one else to.

We usually always milked quite a few cows. In the winter we milked never less than a dozen; In the summer as many as twenty-five. I have known Mrs. Hubbard to come out to the corral on winter mornings and help me milk. It would be around zero. She would milk half of the cows and go to the house and get breakfast while I finished the chores.

I would first get up and build the fire in the cook stove and then go to the corral. George would barely get up for breakfast. After breakfast he would give me my orders. Then he would saddle his horse and go into town. He would come home for dinner then back to town for the afternoon. I really don't know what he did in town. At haying time, branding time, etc. he always hired extra help.

One time we were putting up hay and we had Tyne Arnold helping. Tyne considered himself good at stacking hay and always wanted the job. However, it was just as hard a job as any other in the hay field. Along about 11:00 a.m. old Tyne commenced to look up at the sun, none of us carried watches those days; He would look at the sun then look towards the house. Mrs. Hubbard would wave a dishcloth when it was time to come to dinner. Finally old Tyne could stand it no longer. He stuck his fork in the hay and said, "By God if you are not going to feed us today, give me a drink of water." It wasn't so much what he said, it was the way he said it.

George Hubbard was mean to livestock. If he got irritated with a horse he would beat it over the head. Consequentially all of his horses were head shy. If one would go near their head they would start rearing back or ducking, especially if he came near them. He had a nice black horse. We called him Blackie. He weighed around 1100 pounds. He was very smart and a dandy rope horse.

One morning I roped a coyote off of him. When his rider took down a rope old Blackie knew what to do. This particular morning I was out after some calves, and as I rode up on a small hill there was a coyote eating on a carcass of some kind. I already had my rope back and Blackie was looking to see what I intended to do. When I seen the coyote I hit Blackie and we were on top of the coyote before he seen us. I got my rope on him. We drug him back to the house where I shot him.

One day George was riding Blackie and come down to where we were working. He got off and tied Blackie to a hayrack. When we got the signal to come to dinner he ran right up to the horse, made the horse shy and pull back and broke his bridle reins. George got a hold on his bridle and picked up a pitchfork handle and commenced to beat Blackie over the head. In so doing he knocked the horse's right eye out. You should have heard what we told George. He had ruined the horse.

I worked for the Hubbard's until March 1917. In September 1916 the Hubbard's daughter Helen married Meredith Hughes. More about him later.

We had been real busy all fall getting up feed, branding and working cattle. George sold his calves right on the ranch that year. In other words the buyer received them on the ranch.

After that I was the only hand. I had it all to do. When the weather got bad about Christmas time, we started feeding. I would hitch a team to the hay wagon and haul feed out to the cattle. We had the feed stacked in places around the ranch and fenced in so I was kept pretty busy. George was no help nor was his son. Guy never helped around the place, and at this time he was away at school I believe.

One day I told George that I was finishing the last stack yard. He said, "Well Sunday just throw the gates open and you won't have to feed. I said OK. If that is OK I would like to take the day off. He said fine. I had not had a day off all winter and this was March.

So Sunday I got up early and went out the opening and opened the stack yards so the cattle could get in and clean up what was left of the stacks. I got my horse. I had a very good horse of my own at the time. Saddled him and went to breakfast.

I told George I was going to take a ride up the river to see the Baker boys. More about them later. He said, "I would rather you would hitch up the freight outfit (6 horses and 2 wagons) and go up in Rhodes Canyon to the Morley ranch and get 100 sacks of oil cake (oil cake is a cattle feed made form crushed cotton seed). I told him that in-as-much as we had agreed that I'd be off Sunday I was going to take off and I would get the oil cakes the next day, Monday but I would not do it that day. We were out by the shed at the time. He said, "OK come in the house and get your time" so we went in and figured up what he owed. It came to $11.00. However, he charged me $1.00 a month board for my horse. He was the only man in the country who did that. It was customary for the employer to pasture a man's horse free.

I gathered my war bag and I told him I would pick up my trunk in a day or two. In February 1916 I had sent to Sears Roebuck and got a trunk to keep my belongings in. I still have the trunk, after more than 54 years.

So I crawled on my horse and rode up to the Potters. (About eight miles.)

When I got there Mr. Potter told me to call W.T. Hughes.

This was March 1917.

THE HUGHES'
COLD SPRING RANCH
1917 - 1918

I called Mr. Hughes and he said I heard you and Hubbard called it quits. I told him I was still trying to figure it out. I did not know for sure if I was fired or had quit. He said, "How would you like to come to work for me?" I'll give you $30.00 and keep your horse. I said o.k. I would be at his place in town that afternoon.

I got there early that afternoon and I told him I had to make arrangements to get my trunk so we got in his car and went and got it.

Now Mr. Hughes family consisted, besides his wife, a son, called Meredith. I mentioned he married the Hubbard girl. The Hughes ranch was over on Cold Spring about 25 miles east of Kenton, and about 15 miles northwest of Boise City, Oklahoma. In Cimarron county Oklahoma. This was entirely a cow outfit. Meredith was foreman. Helen, Meredith's wife, did the cooking.

I had now reached the top in ranch hand salaries, $30.00 was top money. It had taken me several years to climb from $5.00 a month. This was typical cow ranch work. Riding fence looking after cattle. If I remember they had about 10,000 acres in this ranch and had about 500 head of cattle.

Mr. Hughes was a fine man, but firm and could be mean if necessary. In the early days he had been a deputy sheriff under Billy Breckenridge, Sheriff of Cochise County,

Arizona during the Tombstone heydays. He also was fair. It was said that he had killed one man. He and Mrs. Hughes lived in Kenton, but he came out to the ranch about once a week.

I had a pretty good bunkhouse where I stayed. However I took my meals with Meredith and Helen. We had all gone to school together.

When Meredith and Helen got married, his parents gave them a Ford car. One day Helen decided she wanted to visit her mother so when Mr. and Mrs. Hughes came over to the ranch the next time she went back to Kenton with them. She was going to be gone a week or so. Meredith said to me, "Smokey lets get a barrel of beer and some liquor." He took out for Clayton and brought back a case of Four Roses, a barrel of Schlitz Beer, a couple of gallons of wine and the saloon keeper gave us a gallon of blackberry cordial.

He left early in the morning and got back just before sundown the same evening. We had a small patch of alfalfa were we kept an extra horse available, should we need him. There was more feed there than the one horse could eat so I had a team hitched to the big mower and was mowing it when he came in. He stopped in front of the bunkhouse. He got out and waved to me to come on over. I drove the team up to the fence and tied them to a post. They were still there the next morning.

First I had to have a beer, he had a dozen extra bottles in a box packed in ice. We decided that maybe the cordial would be a nice drink so we started using one or the other for a chaser.

Our whiskey came in quarts those days ($1.00 per quart). Somehow or other we got some whiskey in with this. However I do know we both got gloriously drunk.

Hughes Town House
Kenton, OK
Circa 1915

The next morning when I came out of the bunkhouse I seen the team still hitched to the mower and tied to the fence so I managed to take care of them. We stayed drunk for several days, but managed to sober up before Mr. and Mrs. Hughes brought Helen back the next Sunday.

We hid the liquor, wine, beer and cordial we had left. We had the Four Roses hid in the hayloft of the barn. I think Mrs. Hughes was suspicious that we had liquor around, because after they went home we found out our whiskey was gone. He told me he thought his mother got our whiskey. He and Helen got in the Ford one night and went to Kenton. He found it under the house and brought it back, without his parents knowing it.

At the time the First World War was going on in Europe, and there was a great demand for horses. One day Mr. Hughes sent us word that he would be out with a horse buyer and for us to have our horses corralled when they got there, so we had them ready. Mr. Hughes designated what horses he wanted to keep and we cut them out and turned them back into the pasture, among those to be sold was a big sorrel. He would weigh about 1000 pounds, but mean as could be. None of us would ride him. We tried working him with the wagon, but he was no good. There was a shed on one side of the corral with a long pole fastened across some of the posts in front. He was in the shed when Mr. Hughes and the buyer was looking him over. He lunged against the pole, knocking it loose and it struck Mr. Hughes across the lower part of the abdomen, which later was to cause him lots of trouble.

There was also a bay horse with the bunch to be sold. I was glad to see him go. He was an ornery devil. He was rough riding and one never knew when he would buck. He used to throw me off every once in a while. I believe he enjoyed throwing me off. When he did he would not run off but would stop and turn towards me and I'll swear at times he looked like he was laughing at me.

When Mr. Hughes was struck on the abdomen it finally turned serious so he went to Kansas City to see a doctor. He had to have an operation on his bladder.

So he was there about six weeks. Meredith and I, with other help branded calves that summer and kept the ranch going while Mr. Hughes was in Kansas City. Meredith and I weaned those calves. Mr. Hughes had a special horse he called Brownie and he told us both to stay off of Brownie. He was a good cutting horse. (Cutting means to separate cattle.)

One day while we were working a herd old Brownie was running loose around there and in the way. Meredith told me to rope him, which I did. He got off the horse he was riding and saddled Brownie and used him to work the herd. Old Brownie was used to the old man, but he was too slow for Meredith so Meredith used his spurs on him and woke him up. Meredith used him for a few days while he needed him. But turned him back out in the pasture before Mr. Hughes came home.

The first thing Mr. Hughes told me when he came back to the ranch was to go get Brownie so I went out and found him and brought him in. He said lets go up in the pasture and find a beef. We found a steer he thought would make good eating but while bringing him in the steer tried to dodge back around Brownie and Brownie had not forgotten the spurring Meredith had given him. Old Brownie headed that steer fast. When he doubled back so swiftly he put Mr. Hughes almost up on the saddle horn. Mr. Hughes pulled Brownie up. I jumped my horse after the steer. Mr. Hughes rode right straight to the house without saying a thing. After we got to the house it was time to go to dinner. We sat down to the table and started eating. Mr. Hughes looked up and said, "Which of you SOB's has been riding my horse. I looked at Meredith and he looked at me. Finally he told his Dad he had been riding Brownie while weaning calves. Mr. Hughes really got on Meredith because he had told us both to stay off his horse. He did not want either of us riding him.

In February 1918 I was called to the service. In the meantime my friend Allen Thornton had joined the army in September 1917 and he was in training in Camp Kearney, California. They brought him home at Christmas time. He died of the flu. I have never forgotten him. He was a good friend. His folks were poor, but wonderful generous people. There was a large family. I believe there was four girls and three boys. His father hauled supplies for the D.K. Lord and Co. store.

More about Meredith. When he came back from Clayton with the liquor he had the front end of the car all tangled up in barbed wire and was running on three rims. Where there was a wire gate in someone's pasture fence he just drove on through.

One time I went to Clayton with a bunch of guys. It was near Christmas. We went to get Christmas liquor. We got several gallons of the barrel whisky in "gallon jugs". A guy by the name of Baker was driving. We got the liquor, but no gas for the car so we got about four miles from home and we run out of gas. We debated as to what we should do as none of us wanted to walk home and that was the closest place to us. Someone suggested putting a gallon of this whisky in the gas tank so that is what we did. We were near the crest of a small hill so we pushed the car up on top and started down the hill and sure enough it took right off. Well that car never ran better and we went right home with it.

End Note

Throughout the rest of dad's life I believe that in his heart the first home he ever really related to was the Potter's. Although he had great relationships with the Jones and several other people like the Williams in Oklahoma he respected and felt closer to the Potters than any of the others. I also believe that this was brought on by the fact that Mrs. Potter was instrumental in him getting some schooling.

In relating the story of Dad coming to the Cimarron Jean M. Burroughs in her book "On the Trail, The Life and Tales of Lead Steer Potter" added the following:

"The other boy, Ed, nicknamed "Sandy", stayed a while then moved on, but Smokey remained much longer, working around the ranch at odd jobs, tending the cattle, and mending fences. When the house became more crowded, Smokey was told that he would have to go to a ranch home that Mrs. Potter had located for him. At the appointed time he was to leave, Smokey was nowhere to be found until someone discovered him, crying his heart out behind the door of a bedroom.

No wonder Smokey wanted to stay. The Potters had good times together. Most of the family were musically inclined and enjoyed singing in the living room around the old pump organ that Mrs. Potter played on occasion."

As was said earlier I'm sure that Dad didn't tell this because it was probably embarrassing to him. It does give us insight into his thoughts of the time however.

It will be noticed that everyone had a nickname except the adults. At this time and for years to come it was unheard of for a young person to address an adult or an older person by their first name; however, nicknames were a way of life for the school age people.

Mr. Potter had a fantastic history. As Dad mentioned he had driven cattle from Abilene, Texas to Dodge City, Kansas on the Old Chisholm Trail. I was told he also fought Indians. He was generally known in later years as "Colonel Jack". The Governor of New Mexico bestowed the "Colonel" title on him as an honorary title. Jack Potter was a trail boss at the age of 18, served three terms in the New Mexico State Legislature and was elected as Justice of the Peace in Clayton. He wrote several stories about his trail driving experiences that were compiled into books. He was also the subject of a piece of cowboy poetry "Jack Potter's Courtin'" by the noted poet S. Omar Barker.

As Dad said, Mr. Potter was a very large man and Mrs. Potter was tiny, especially in comparison. You could tell even when we visited the Potter's in 1948 that he worshipped the ground she walked on. When she got tired and decided to *go to bed he, very gently walked up and picked her up and kissed her goodnight and just as gently set her back on the floor. He was eighty-four years old at the time and did it with no effort.*

There was a story about Mr. Potter's father. It seems as though he was an itinerant preacher and when he would start preaching if anyone in the congregation would make any remarks or tend to get rowdy he would pull out two six shooters and shoot candles out on each side of the room at the same time. He would then tell the congregation that he was going to "bring fire and brimstone into their lives one way or another, which way would they like it". I would imagine that there were very few remarks after that.

Book Four

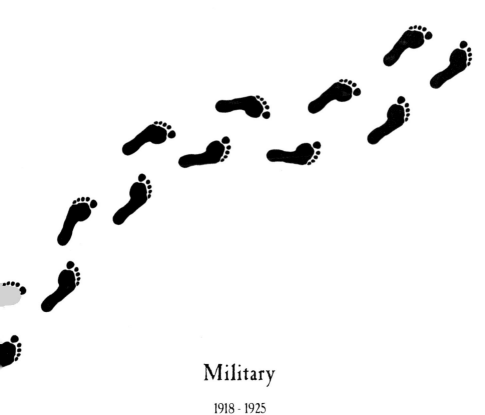

Military

1918 - 1925

THE ARMY
1918 - 1919

On Feb. 24, 1918 I entered the service at Boise City, Oklahoma. There were 22 of us. We had to go to Dalhart, Texas to entrain for Camp Travis, Texas. When we left Boise City it was still winter. Camp Travis is near to San Antonio and we found everything like spring. The trees were leafed out nice and green and the weather was warm.

The first planes I ever saw was while we were en route to Camp Travis, Texas. We stopped at Fort Worth and the army had an airfield there and they were training with some of the old two wing jobs.

When we arrived we were placed under quarantine for 21 days to find out if any of us would come down with any communicable disease. We were given a vaccination for small pox, shots for typhoid and of course we were starting to get our uniforms. The first pieces of uniform we got were a hat and an overcoat. They started to teach us soldiering, how to drill, salute, etc.

I had only been there a few days when I got the whooping cough and along with the typhoid shots it was rough. It seemed as if about the time our 21 days was over someone would come down with something and we would be stuck for another 21, like me with whooping cough. It is rough to get whooping cough when you are 21 years old.

One day we were called out for formation and divided up into squads. We were told to get our gear, by this time we had all our uniforms and had disposed of our civilian clothes. We were to return to the same squads. We were marched off to what we thought would be our outfits. I was assigned to Co. F 357 infantry. I was there only about a week and along

123

with some others was told to pack up and fall out into formation. It was about the middle of the afternoon. We had all our clothes etc. in large cloth bags called Barracks bags. We sat around all the rest of the afternoon on these bags. Finally they told us to come to supper, eat and go right back. About dark a couple of officers told us to pick up our bags and fall in. We marched about 1.5 miles and we saw some railroad coaches. We were ordered aboard, and were assigned berths, two men to the lowers and one to the uppers. When all got loaded we were ordered to turn off all lights and pull down the blinds and we rolled out. We had no idea where we were going so we went to bed. The porter came through and instructed us how to make up out beds. Gave us sheets and pillowcases. We had our own issued blankets, two each.

The next morning we were in the yards at Houston. I forgot to mention we were assigned guard duty. We were given clubs and we took turns guarding each end of the coach, and told not to let anyone on or off the train, except the crew of course.

We got up and straightened out our berths and put them up and commenced to wonder about breakfast, but that was soon solved. They had placed two express cars in the train, one near the rear end and one not far from the front. We were told to get our mess kits and line up. As I was nearer the front end of the train so I lined up with the gang going forward. After eating we would clean out mess kits in a large G.I. can in the car vestibule.

We still did not know were we were going. Of course there was lots of rumors. Some said we were going to New Orleans to catch a ship for Europe, but none of us had had enough training as yet for front line service. Some said we were going to Panama to guard the canal.

Since leaving the Cimarron none of this had bothered me, however when we got to the place where we crossed the Mississippi River, I believe it was Baton Rouge, La. It was during the night I woke up and looked out window and they were pushing the coach on the train ferry. Somehow it gave me a nostalgic feeling. I was getting farther from my old stomping grounds than I had ever been.

A day or so later we came to a place called DeFuniak Springs, Fla. We were unloaded there and exercised. The town was built around a nice lake. We marched around the lake. The reason I remember this so well is... Some time before I had a subscription to a magazine and there was an ad in it. Land for sale at this place. 10 acre plots for $10.00 an acre. It interested me so I asked Mr. Hughes what he thought of it and said he thought it was a swindle. While I was there that day I talked to a native about it. He said it was no swindle. It was an estate that was being sold to satisfy the heirs. He said the $10.00 an acre land was cut over pine forest, but well worth what was asked for it and had all been sold.

It was Easter Sunday morning when we arrived at our destination, Camp Joseph E. Johnston, Fla. Our train pulled into the camp just after daylight.

We detrained and was marched about a mile to a place in the woods on the banks of the St. Johns River. There was a street laid out all paved and guttered, but nothing on either side but pinewoods and palmetto shrubs. We were stopped along the street and told to be at ease. We were hungry. We'd had no breakfast yet.

After a while some trucks came along and dumped off some pyramid tents. They will handle about five people also some cots. We were to clean off the ground and set up our camp. Oh yes, they also dropped off some shovels and rakes.

Finally they brought us a large cook tent, stove, everything to cook and feed us, but it was late afternoon before we got anything to eat. Then we had a spoon-full of grits, two prunes and one slice of bread, but we did have plenty of coffee. Some of us who had lived in the west had to learn the art of living in a tent in a moist sandy country.

The ground was sandy and it was not hard to drive a tent peg in the ground. When we put up our tents we put them up real tight. We had them all lined up in nice straight rows, but the next morning most of them were down. We did not think that during the night we would have real heavy dew and the ropes and canvas would shrink and pull up the pegs. After the first night there we learned to loosen our guy ropes when we turned in.

There were a lot of alligators in the river at that place between sundown and dark one could look out over the river and see just their eyes sticking up out of the water like frogs sometime do, only the distance between their eyes was much wider.

Just east of us there was a bunch of Negro troops. Boy, they were really afraid of the gators.

We were not allowed out. We could not leave camp so they set up camp guards. We had no guns. We were furnished clubs somewhat like the police carry. We had orders not to let anyone out of our camp. Anyone in uniform could come in, but no one could go out.

There was a bunch of fellows, "farmer boys", from Illinois that came in the next day and a certain rivalry sprung up between us. We started calling them "apple knockers." They were mostly from southern Illinois, coal miners, etc. I learned later that those people from that area are called "apple knockers" because they do raise lots of apples there.

Corporal Alfred H. Phillips
Sinzig, Germany - 1919

We worked on our camp until we really had a nice looking place, a regular park. Visitors from Jacksonville would come out and walk there, and remark how pretty it was. We built a nice path along the river and around through the woods.

We found out that alligators liked dogs. Every stray dog we could get we would tie up after dark to a tree on the edge of the river. The next morning the dog would be gone. Many a family pet disappeared at that camp.

One day a couple of officers lined us up. One of them started calling out names. When our name was called we formed another line. Then we were told to get our gear and follow them. We were marched to some wooden barracks. The next day we were given our official designation, "The 306 Field Remount Squadron".

A few days later we moved into tents again in another part of the camp. There we started our training. The learning to be a soldier was fine but we were given a bunch of horses and we were supposed to be trained on how to handle horses. It did not take us but a couple of days to find out the officers we had, except for a couple, did not know a thing about horses.

At first they issued us regular stock saddles. Then they started to show us how to saddle a horse. Some of us started to laugh and this one guy got mad at us and started to bawl us out. It so happened we had an old time cavalry sergeant who told him where we came from so he finally said, "All right, let me see you saddle a horse. All he had to go on was some book on horses, so when we showed him how he was satisfied. We also showed him we could ride. I believe it was sometime around the middle of April when the outfit was formed.

I had not been paid since entering the army, so the first of May, or the thirteenth of April in other words, I got paid. They were issuing passes so I got a weekender (Saturday noon until Monday morning) pass and went to Jacksonville. I met three other guys and we hired a car to take us to St. Augustine. We spent Sunday down there. We got back to camp about midnight Sunday night.

We were issued the old Enfield rifles. There was four outfits near each other, the 305, 306, 307, and the 308 Field Remount Squadrons. Each outfit was a unit of its own. We mounted our own guard. Each outfit was completely independent of the other.

If we wanted to go to town, Jacksonville was about ten miles away. There was taxis running all the time it only cost 50 cents each way into town. Sometimes if we could not get a pass we would slip out, if we could get by the guard. That was not hard to do because the guard was usually one of your buddies. One night I slipped out and went to town and did not get back until about 3:00 a.m. The next morning when reveille blew and I did not hear it. When I woke up the platoon sergeants were reporting. I was in second platoon. I heard Sergeant Rountree report, "Second platoon all present and accounted for". I slipped out of my cot and was putting on my clothes when who popped in but the First Sergeant O'Rourke. He looked at me and said, "Well, what the hell are you doing in here?" I was all dressed and was putting on my last shoe. I told him I had to drop out and see what was wrong with my shoe. I must have had a rock in it. He said, "a rock is it, get your fatigues (work clothes) on and report to the kitchen."

Besides our regular company cook we had one cook especially for the officers. He was a Greek. His name was Lyman Lymberry from Corpus Christi, Texas. He had a space in the supply tent for his equipment. On this day he baked two coconut custard pies for the officer's mess. There was another guy on K.P. with me. I can't recall his name off hand.

At any rate this other K.P. and I ate both of those pies, that day. Boy was he a mad Greek. He never did get over that. He never found out until we were discharged who ate the pies. He and I got to be very good friends and every time he got a few drinks in him he would say he would like to know who took the pies.

About the first of June we commenced packing our equipment and I was called up to the Captain's Office. He asked me if I had ever had any experience handling men. Up to that time I really hadn't so I told him I had always been a ranch hand. Well, he said, "I am going to promote you to Corporal".

I guess this would be a good time to name as many of our officers as I can remember. We had six officers, Captain Mordecai, 1st Lieutenant Harrison, 1st Lieutenant Dr. D. H. Garrison. We also had a 1st Lieutenant of Veterinary. Also two other line lieutenants, but I cannot off hand remember their names. The non-commissioned officers and men are not too necessary for this story, so as I go along I will only mention their names if their names have an interest to the story.

About the first of June we got orders to start getting ready to leave. We commenced to pack everything we were to take with us. One day about the middle of the month we were told to make up field packs and be ready to pull out. Field packs consisted of blankets, extra shoes, underwear, shirts, trousers, socks, mess gear, cartridge belt, rifle, bayonet, helmet, gas mask, etc. Early one morning we marched down to the railroad yards. There was some Pullman coaches waiting, we were told we would have to hurry but, as usual, it was the old army game. Hurry up and wait. We stood around there until nearly noon before we boarded the train. Immediately we posted a guard on each end of the car, no one was allowed to board or leave the train. Well, we finally pulled out and as before there was three men to a berth, two down and one up. Inasmuch as I was a non-com I rated to sleep in a lower.

We did not know it at the time but we were on our way to Camp Hill, Virginia, Port of embarkation for overseas.

On our way we stopped early one morning in Richmond, Va. I had a window open on my side. When the train stopped I looked out and there was a man standing there. I asked what place is this? He said, "Richmond, Virginia." At the same time he reached in his hip pocket and pulled out a pint of whisky and asked if I wanted it. I told him sure. Here I will give it to you, so you can pass it around. I have always liked Richmond, Virginia even though I have never been back there since.

We were coming from Florida and were wearing summer uniforms so when we arrived in Camp Hill they had us turn in those light clothes and issued us wool uniforms.

On the 29th of June 1918 we marched down to Newport News, Va. and boarded the army transport U.S.S. Tenedores. The troops were ordered aboard in companies. As each company approached the gangway their co-commander called each soldier in his outfit by name. As his name was checked he went aboard. There were sailors stationed at intervals that directed us on. My outfit went down in the hold, about four decks down. There were makeshift bunks down there. They were four high. I was wise enough to get a top bunk. I was glad I did after we got out to sea.

The whole area had a smell that we were not used to, dampness, tar, oakum, and human. Especially after the ship started to roll. Most of us got seasick. We sailed the afternoon of the thirtieth of June. It took us until the afternoon of the 13th of July to get to Brest, France.

They had us soldiers doing lookout duty even in the crow's nest on each mast. We must have gone way north because for a few days we had very little darkness. One could read a newspaper at two o'clock in the morning.

The first day out we had only a few transports and two or three Navy vessels, "destroyers," with us. The next day a large convoy fell in with us. We later learned that they had come out of New York. There were many more destroyers, also a cruiser. I believe it was the U.S.S. Chicago. These navy ships stayed with us until we were about half way over. A fleet out of European bases met us. They convoyed us on in.

FRANCE
1918

We anchored in the harbor in Brest, France on the afternoon of 13 July 1918. Over on the shore was a series of rather high hills and there were roads winding around up the hills. Some one started singing, "There is a long long trail a winding" and all took it up. There were ships loaded with troops all around us and it seemed as if they were all singing. It was beautiful. There must have been at least 10,000 voices singing.

July 14th is France's National holiday, "Bastille Day" so some outfits were assigned to help unload our ship. There were several carloads of frozen beef in the lower holds. As we could not dock they had to use lighters to take the meat ashore so we did not leave the ship until the fifteenth.

Then they hiked us out in the country about four miles and we pitched our pup tents in a field. We were only there two or three days when we were routed out early one morning and told we only had a short time to get down to town to entrain for other parts. Now be it understood we were never told where we were going. When we started out we just went. If we were told to get on a train we got on the train. If it was a ship so be it.

We rushed around and got to the yards by 9:00 a.m. and it was after 9:00 p.m. before we entrained. We stayed in those railroad yards all day and we were not allowed to leave the immediate area.

Finally a train of French boxcars came in; these boxcars were called "40 men – 8 horses." We were loaded on. There were some benches in the cars but they took up so much space that it did not take us long to throw them out

133

after we got to rolling. We just sat on our packs or lay on the car floor just any way we could.

Somewhere along the line we picked up a dog. I think he was a "Heinz 57 Variety" breed. At any rate everyone was tired and trying to sleep. I was sitting in the door with my feet hanging out. All at once I heard a yelp in back of me. It seems as if one of the boys I think his name was Bill Smith, was laying stretched out on the floor sound asleep and the dog came along and stuck his foot in Bill's mouth. Bill must have been sleeping with his mouth open. Bill closed his mouth and bit the dog so he raised up and caught the dog and threw him off the train. That was the last we saw of the dog.

The next day we pulled into a place called St. Nazaire. We hiked out to what was known as camp #1. We settled in some old French barracks there. The first thing we had to do was get our hair cut short. Many of us had our heads clipped, a French barber came through camp. All he had was a comb, scissors, a pair of hand clippers and a box to sit on.

We were supposed to get paid on the last day of the month, but we sailed on the 30th of June and we were not paid. All the money I had on me was a nickel and I carried that all the way to camp- #1.

One day I was laying in my bunk taking a nap and someone asked me if I would take a chance on a violin. Incidentally we were all broke. This old boy needed money and he was out of another outfit. He said the chances were 5 cents. I gave him my last nickel, rolled over and went back to sleep. In a little while someone was shaking me and saying something about me having a violin. I told him I had no violin. "Well," he said, "you have now." I later sold it for about $5.00.

We moved into town. St. Nazaire is right on the coast where we took over a remount base from the French. Our duty was to receive horses, as they were unloaded off ships coming from the U.S. We stayed there about six weeks.

I was working a detail in the corrals one day and along with some other officers came old General John J. "Blackjack" Pershing himself.

Some of us went into the downtown section of St. Nazaire one day and we seen a sign, "Cheyenne Charlie's Bar" so we thought we would stop in and see what it was like. There were women waitresses and bar maids there, but the man running the place looked familiar. I asked him if he had ever tended bar for Carl Eklund in Clayton, New Mexico. It came about that we had a lot in common. He had worked for Eklund also Tom Grey, another saloonkeeper in Clayton. While I did not know him personally, he knew people I did. After that he never charged me for drinks. He assured me I was welcome at anytime, and not to be embarrassed about the free drinks. Every time I went there his girls would set a quart of Scotch whisky on the table. Sometime I would drink scotch, but most times I was content with just beer. If I went by myself he did not particularly like it and always told me to bring a friend or two.

About the first of September we loaded out again. As usual we had no idea where we were going. Another outfit came in and we turned all the horses we had over to them. We felt we were headed for the front.

One morning our train stopped in some yard. We were riding French 3rd class passenger cars at the time. We could smell fresh baked bread and it sure smelled good. Finally we spotted it. There was a French Army bakery a short distance away. Some of us thought we would investigate. When we got over there they were loading a French boxcar with fresh baked bread. The car was along side a loading platform. We crawled under the platform and reached up between the edge of it and the car and right within reach we were able to grab a loaf of bread. Their bread was baked in round loaves. We would wait until the Negro who was loading the car would unload his cart in the car and go back to the shop for more, then grab a loaf and run. Usually when we were moving we were on short rations and always hungry. The bread tasted real good. Finally some of the gang got caught so they shut the car door until we left.

Eventually we arrived at a placed called Toule and hiked out to some old French barracks, called Marshal Ney. They were old French artillery barracks. We then received horses that had been shipped to us from all over France. At Toule we were close enough to the front that we could hear the guns. We could also see aerial battles and we came under bombing a couple of times, although we were never hit.

I have not explained why we had the horses. At that time nearly all transportation depended on horse drawn equipment. We did have trucks, cars, etc., but they were no good near the front as there were no roads. And if a motor vehicle got off the road it was done for. It was usually muddy and the ground was boggy. We moved horses to the front, brought out sick or crippled ones to dispose of, or cure. We turned those over to a veterinary outfit. We were there until the armistice was signed.

I will never forget that day. There was a continuous roar of big and small guns for days. All at once it ceased. The silence cannot be explained. I have heard it said that the silence was deafening, but I am sure that does not explain it.

That evening the captain told us he would not hold us responsible for anything we did for the next 24 hours. He did say he hoped there would be enough of us around to care

136

for what we had. We went into town. Every Frenchman we seen had a bottle and one had to drink with him. There was a period of time, oh at least a couple of days that I don't know what happened and even then I was in a sort of daze for over a week.

One day I was told to take a detail of men and go to the railhead for food supplies. The supply sergeant went along. In other words we went with him. We got a supply of food. Finally the ration sergeant of the supply dump told me to take my men and wagon and go to a car and get a quarter of beef. After getting the beef we were to meet our supply sergeant at a certain place in town.

We drove to the car and there was no one there and the door was out of sight of the supply dump sergeant. We got ten quarters instead of one. We had a cover on the wagon so it could not be seen.

Our supply sergeant said after he saw what we had done. "Boy, if that guy at the dump catches up with us we will all go to the brig." However there were other people who got meat right after we did. In fact there were several wagons pulled up as we were leaving. We were lucky to be by ourselves when we were loading the beef. It came to good use before we got any more.

One day before the armistice was signed I was in Toule. I went into a place for a beer and I sat down at a table with a French soldier. He could talk some English and he had a bottle of wine he asked me to share it with him. I bought him a beer. Wine was just about the same as beer. It was not long until we were both feeling good. That was when he gave me a cigarette lighter he had made from a German "Minniewurffer" shell. I still have the lighter.

Another time I was walking down the street in Toule and I heard someone say, 'Hey, Corporal." I looked across the street and a 1st Lieutenant was waving me to come across the street. I went over and he said, "Do you know where I could find Lieutenant General Hennessey?" It took a minute for it to soak in so I said, "Yes, come on." He had just come out of the lines so I took him into a place and bought a bottle of Three Star Hennessey Cognac. He had not been paid and he was thirsty. I don't remember to this day how I got back to the outfit.

During the St. Mihiel offensive we got orders to deliver a trainload of horses to an artillery outfit near Belfort on the Swiss border, in the Vosges Mountains. We loaded eight horses to a car with one man to each car. The trip down there was uneventful. After we loaded and turned them over to the artillery outfit and were ready to start back to our base, we found ourselves hard pressed for transportation. However after waiting nearly twenty-four hours we did get out. Our officer along with a colonel from the artillery prevailed on the local train officials to put a coach on a freight train going our way.

Now, anyone who has never ridden a French train in wartime has missed a treat. They don't run on schedule and one never knows when he will get to his destination. It only took us over night to go from Toule to Belfort, but coming back it took us nearly 36 hours. We expected to get back as fast as we went so we were only given two cans of corned beef, one can of tomatoes for each two men and a box of hard tack. Before noon the next day those rations were gone. We would roll a while and then we would pull up on a siding and sit there for a couple of hours.

The French shipped their red wine in hogsheads, on flat cars. It so happened we stopped on the next track to a train with some of the wine cars. We got the idea we could get some of this wine. We could smell it seeping through the pores of the wood. We all carried 45 caliber automatics so we just shot a hole in the side of a hogshead and one in the top and filled our canteens. After we got what we wanted, even both officers, a Lieutenant by the name of Worth and the Veterinary officer, we whittled a couple of wooden plugs and stopped the leaks. After we did that it did not take long for the train to move and it didn't take long to get to Toule. We had hardly anything to eat when we got the wine and we were all getting pretty well wound up while filling our canteens. That plus having a full quart to finish up, we were really loaded when we got in, officers and all.

GERMANY
1918

I must mention while on our march into Germany we spent Thanksgiving at a place called Conflons Jarny in Northern France. The Germans had occupied this place for several years and had farmed some of it. There were several fields of cabbage around there so for Thanksgiving dinner in 1918 we had boiled cabbage, English hard tack and coffee.

A few days after the Armistice was signed we got orders to move again. It was the 16th of Nov. This time we took horses with us. We rode one and led two. We went up through the St. Mihiel and the Argonne. We caught up with the Germans near the Luxembourg border. We had to hold up at a place called Battenberg, in Luxembourg until they got out of our way.

At a place called Trier we crossed the Moselle River into Germany on November 30, 1918. We were among the first U.S. troops to enter Germany. We hiked into the city of Trier the last day of November in 1918. We really did not know what was going to happen to us as we rode down through the streets of the city. I expected the Germans, who were left there to start shooting, but there was no young men there. Only women, kids and old men and they were hungry.

We camped at what had been a dairy, but there were no cows there at the time. We had to kill a horse because he was gassed. We asked the old man who was taking care of the place where we could dispose of him. He said he would be glad to take care of it. They skinned and ate that horse. Women and kids carried big chunks of that meat away in pans.

From there we followed the Moselle River downstream toward the Rhine. The Moselle River Valley is beautiful, high hills on both sides all terraced with grape vineyards covering the hillsides. They make some of the world's best wines, Moselle red and Moselle white wines are some of the best.

We were traveling on the south side of the river, so on the second day after leaving Trier we crossed over on a pontoon bridge at a place called Cochim. We were using mules on our wagons so in crossing this bridge a lead mule got scared and jumped off the bridge into deep water. I happened to be near so I cut him loose from the wagon as he was getting tangled in his harness. One of the officers came up and asked why I cut him loose. I told him to give the mule a chance to swim out, which he did. Then he gave me hell for cutting the harness. I asked him if he would rather of lost the mule and harness or just have to repair the harness.

We spent the night at Cochim and about everyone got drunk on Moselle wine. The next day we went into the town called Mayen, but only stayed there over night.

On December 16th one month after leaving Toule, France we got to our destination, a small slate mining village called Mosella-Schacht. Here we spent the rest of the winter. We lived in the German houses, each house had to furnish as much room as they possibly could for us.

A fellow by the name of Schwartz and I had a room on the third floor of a house occupied by a family by the name of Nolte. They had two young daughters about 10 and 11 years old. They were pretty nice to us and we to them. Mrs. Nolte would wash our clothes for what soap there would be left. Schwartz and I would steal bacon and sugar out of the kitchen and bring it to them whenever we could. Mrs. Nolte kept our rooms clean, blankets washed, etc.

On the march in there we camped at times where German and French troops had camped and we all got lousy but Mrs. Nolte soon cleaned us up. Schwartz and I would buy wine and steal sugar from the kitchen and give it to Mr. Nolte so every morning about a half hour before reveille he would come wake us up with a couple of glasses, like our tumblers. He would have them half full of wine with a teaspoon of sugar. Then he would fill them with hot water. Of course we always had to have him have one with us. We had lots of snow on the ground that winter and it got pretty cold. We was out in it all the time, but neither Schwartz nor I caught even a cold but when spring came our faces were really red.

About the first of April a directive came out saying that there was a motor school to be started at a place called Brohl. Brohl was about 50 kilometer from where we were so I put in for it. I did not know anything about automobile motors and wanted to learn. Also it gave me a change of scenery. There was several German trucks there, but all had been more or less disabled. Timing had been changed so they would not fire. They all operated off a magneto, and they did have the best magneto made at that time, "The Bosch".

We were attending classes in the morning and fooling around with the trucks in the afternoon. They had no rubber tires. Some of them had just plain iron wagon tires, others had double tires, an iron tire shrunk on the wheel with a large tire and large coil springs between them. They all had enclosed cabs over the driver's seat and all kinds of lockers, cupboards, gun racks, drawers, etc.

One day I found a lemon type hand grenade in one of the drawers. It was a dud. I was standing out in front of one of the trucks and looking at the hand grenade when I dropped it. Just as it hit the ground the truck behind me backfired. Well it just scared the devil out of me. I was sure that grenade had gone off. We learned a lot and got the trucks running. We also did a lot of goofing off.

While we were there I met a man that had come over from the 201st engineers. He was a "mess sergeant" named Ray Covo. He was from Fall River, Mass. More about him later.

When the six weeks were up we went back to our outfits. My outfit had moved to a place across the Rhine River from Coblenz called Ehrenbrietstein. We stayed right on the river in an old German Artillery barracks. This was not a bad place. Coblenz was a nice large city and there was plenty to do there.

In July we were ordered to move again. This time to a place about 35 kilometers from Coblenz to a place called Kripp. There was four outfits there, the 301, 303, 305 and 306 remount squadrons. We commenced to receive horses from all over the occupied territory. At one time we had more than 2,000 head of horses and mules. When outfits started going home they turned their horses over to us. We were to dispose of them. We sold them to anyone who would buy them. We sold some to the British, French, Polish, and Belgians. We also sold a lot to individuals. Many of them went for food. A good deal of horsemeat is eaten in Europe. I ate it, but it is more red and coarser than beef, maybe a little sweeter.

Summer along the Rhine was enjoyable. The weather did not seem to be too hot. There were fruit trees all along the roads, apples, peaches, plums and all you had to do was stop and help yourself. They also grow some of the nicest strawberries you ever saw.

We had to patrol Kripp as it was on the edge of the occupied zone. It was on the rivers edge, and just across the river was the unoccupied zone. The people who lived on our side where not allowed to go over to the other side without a permit. That also applied to those on the other side who wanted to come over our way.

There was a man who ran a saloon on our side who would slip over on the other side and get his liquor. We only patrolled from 6:00 a.m. until midnight. We had a room where we stayed from midnight until morning. One night we caught him coming in with his boat loaded with liquor. He had to unload his barrels on the shore and roll them about a block to his place of business. We watched him go into his shop then we went the other way with a smaller barrel. We hid it in some bushes along the river. The next day we had the boys who were cleaning corrals with a wagon pick it up. It was about 15 gallons of good cognac. We took it up to the outfit. We had some times until it was gone. That did not take long.

In Feb. of 1919 we were given a chance for leave. We could go to Paris for five days not counting travel time or go to a place in the south of France called Auxeles Bains. I chose Paris.

A few of us started out. We first had to go to Coblenz as we were stationed near Mayen at the time. In Coblenz we caught a troop train called a leave train. We rode that thing all night and all day the next day and all night again and we were still not in Paris. We also had to forage for our food. The second morning we came to a French camp. We got off the train and went over there. We seen a line up of French soldiers and found out that there was a sort of canteen there where we could buy crackers, sardines, and bottles of wine. We got in line, but we did not seem to be getting anywhere.

145

We finally saw why. Those damn frogs were slipping in ahead of us.

There was only five or six of us and too many for us to jump. We were really mad, but what could we do. However, luck was with us, a French Major who could talk English came along and stopped and talked to us. It did not take him long to see what was going on. He asked us how long we had been in line. We told him about an hour. Boy, he called that line to attention and I could not understand what he said, but we were ushered up to the head of the line. We got plenty of food. Our train was still over on a siding. We asked him if we could get a faster train into Paris. He told us there was a Paris express due through later in the day. We walked to a town about three kilometers away where the train stopped. We didn't try to buy a ticket, because it was a first class train and enlisted men would not be sold a ticket. We were only supposed to ride in second and third class trains so we climbed aboard without tickets. After we got on and the train was rolling the conductor came through. Boy, did he set up a howl! But again, we could not savvy French. We did find out how much our fare would be and paid him in cash. That satisfied him.

It only took us about a couple of hours to get to Paris. We never did see the troop train again. We reported into leave headquarters and got our papers. We were told when we were to leave Paris. My partner was a fellow from Datil, New Mexico by the name of McPhaul.

We got a room in a place called Family Hotel in what was known as Saint Denis District. We went everywhere anyone recommended us to see. Saw most places of interest.

One night we were returning to our quarters after seeing a local show and as we started in to the hotel a couple of Australian soldiers stopped us and asked for the loan of five francs each. They said they would see us and pay us back the next morning. They asked us what was our room number and we told them. We gave them the ten francs. We never expected to see them again. Early the next morning they brought a couple of bottles of cognac and paid us our money. I have liked Australians ever since.

About the first of November 1919 we were told we would soon return to the U.S. We had to pack everything we would turn in there to give to whoever relieved us. On Thanksgiving Day we left Germany and returned to Brest, France. We had to go through a sort of staging process, also take physical examinations, turn in all our French money and get paid in American money. We were paid all we had coming. We were there nearly two weeks getting cleared.

We finally boarded the U.S.S. Powhatan, a troop transport. It took us 14 days to get to New York. It was a rough crossing. I got real seasick. We were on the second deck. To go down to our quarters we had to go forward through the well deck. The galley was in the forepeak amidships. There was a passageway alongside the galley.

One day another guy and I were on our way below and as we passed the door of the galley there was a box of hot boiled franks sitting there. We picked it up and went below with it. The galley door was closed so the cooks did not see us. These franks I suppose were for the crews mess. We got down in our compartment in a corner out of sight. I almost foundered myself eating franks. I had been seasick and had not eaten very much and they tasted so good. I got over my seasickness right then. I have liked boiled franks ever since.

We arrived in Hoboken, N.J. on the 20th of Dec. 1919. I was assigned a detail and was told to get the company baggage when it was unloaded, and bring it to Fort Dix, New Jersey.

The baggage was not available until the next day. That night I went ashore. Right across the street at the end of the dock was a café. I walked over there and in the window was the most beautiful coconut custard pie one ever seen. I had not eaten a piece of pie since we left the states. I went in and asked the waitress how much she wanted for that pie. I believe she said 75 cents. I told her to bring it on and coffee with it. I ate the whole pie. It sure was good and I still like coconut custard pie.

We got our baggage off the ship and on to a train the next day. We went to Fort Dix. On Dec. 24, 1919 I received my discharge from the army. It was snowing at the time so four other fellows and myself hired a man to drive us to Camden, just across the Delaware River from Philadelphia where I caught the train to Clayton, New Mexico.

RETURN HOME
1919

I went to the railroad station and bought a ticket to Clayton, New Mexico. Also got a berth on a Pullman to Chicago. I asked for a lower, but could only get an upper berth.

The train pulled out about 11:00 P.M. but I never seen who had the lower berth until the next morning when I returned from breakfast. By that time the berths were made up and I found that the occupant was a U.S. Navy Chief Petty Officer. I later learned his name was Hallahan, a chief carpenters mate.

This was Christmas morning and we stopped awhile in Pittsburgh. We had to change trains in Chicago from the Pennsylvania line to the Santa Fe line. When I asked for a lower berth to La Junta, Colo. I could only get an upper. Again I got Hallahan for a berth partner. More about Hallahan later.

At La Junta I had to change trains and take a local to Trinidad then stay overnight to get a Colorado and Southern train into Clayton.

I arrived in Clayton about noon on the 27th of Dec. 1919. I got my dinner and started a walk down the street to look the town over and who did I meet but Mr. Tooker.

I walked up to him and asked him if he knew me. I was still in uniform. He said yes. I asked him if he remembered whipping me with a buggy whip and I asked would he like to try whipping me again. I also asked him if he was man enough. We went around the corner off the main street on a side street. I took off my overseas cap and slapped him across the face with it. He put his arms over his face and whimpered like a baby. I called him a damned coward and walked off.

I went to find a telephone to call Kenton and was told to go to the telephone office. There I ran into Ed Geer's cousin Dora McClary. She had not heard from Ed for years. She was working at the office. I called the Hughes and told them I would be in Kenton the next day. The next day I went to Kenton on the mail stagecoach.

While I was gone Mr. Hughes got one of the Cochran boys to take my place, Clarence the son of George Cochran. He understood I would get my job back when I returned so I went back to Cold Springs. My salary was to be $45.00 a month. This was Jan. 1920.

In June we branded calves and when that was done I asked to be off for a couple of weeks. I was getting restless. When I first got back I was glad to settle down and get away from people. I had been back six months and I felt as if I must do something.

I went to Lawton to see my sisters. I had been gone 13 years and this was the first time I had seen them. They were living with their father, Mr. Dauner. He started to give me a long tale of woe about how hard it was to raise two girls. Of course he was right because they were only 8 and 10 years when our mother died.

He started to make apologies for me leaving home in 1907. It finally wound up by me letting him know that I felt he was responsible for the whole thing.

I have always felt glad that it all came about as it did. I only spent a few days there and I returned to the Cimarron Country. I stayed at the ranch until the fall work was finished. Then I resigned and went back to Lawton.

As I said I was restless and had come to realize that there was no future working on a cow ranch unless one owned it so I made arrangements with the Hughes to take care of my equipment until such time that I could send for it. I had sold my horse. They sold my saddle, etc.

I went back to Lawton intending to find out what I could do in town in 1920-1921. I got a job at the cotton oil mill, the same one where I got in trouble years before. I found a place to board. The folk's name was Daniels. They had a boy who was in the Navy during the war. He had served on a destroyer on the West coast. He told me a lot about the Navy.

I managed to make a living and got by the winter. Work was getting scarcer and I saw I would have to do something else so on the 24th of April I went down to Dallas, Texas and joined the Navy.

THE NAVY
1921 - 1925

Bob Daniels had told me of the possibilities of retirement after 20 or 30 years in the navy. I made up my mind that that might be a place for me, at least there was a future.

When I arrived at the recruiting office I met a chief machinist mate. He told me to ask to be enlisted as a fireman, not a seaman. Of course I did not know anything about the difference, but when he said as a fireman I would draw $48.00 a month against $36.00 as a seaman I knew the difference.

I asked to be enlisted as a fireman and I was sent to the navy receiving station at New Orleans, La. There I got my sea bag and was indoctrinated into navy life.

I did not have to take recruit training because I had basic military training in the army, however I did have to take all my vaccinations and typhoid shots again.

The commandant was a Captain Macomb. Every morning he held quarters in what was called the sail loft and we had to sing the first verse of the Star Spangled Banner.

One day while I was there we were asked if there was anyone who knew infantry drill. I foolishly held up my hand with some others. I was picked to drill some reserve officers, who were putting in their two weeks duty and were to put in a certain amount of drill time. They were mostly special duty officers, doctors, accountants, engineers, etc. There was about 20 of them, Ensigns, Lieutenants Jr. grade and Lieutenants.

It looked funny to see me, a third class fireman, drilling them. They were good sports and took my orders well and thanked me personally when it was over. I suppose they had their orders previously.

On May 30th we were assigned to march in the Memorial Day parade. It was to take place on Canal Street in New Orleans. We would march from the river to City Park, about 20 or more blocks. We were to help dedicate a monument donated to the park in honor of the men from that area that had served in WW1. It sure was hot that day and the humidity was high. We were wet with perspiration when we arrived at the park.

We formed three sides of a square, the army on one side, marines on one side and the navy across the end in between with the statue in front of us. The monument was covered and the cover was arranged so that if a rope was pulled the cover would fall down.

The daughter of the mayor of New Orleans was to uncover the statue and was to pull the rope at a signal. When the cover fell we were to fire a salute. First the army, then the marines and last us.

This young lady was a beautiful girl about 18 or so, but when the firing ceased there was a small pool of water under her feet. Every time a volley was fired she would jump. I really don't believe the water at her feet was perspiration.

I was told by some people there that if I wanted a good ship to put in for a destroyer. Every day a request would come in for men for some ships. We watched the bulletin board. One day a request came in for men for a destroyer. It was the U.S.S. Stribling (DD-96) so I put in for it and was assigned to it. She was supposed to be in the navy yard at Charleston, S.C.

154

They sent about twenty-five of us up there but when we arrived in Charleston she had sailed so we boarded the U.S.S. Foote (DD-158) for transfer to the Stribling.

Dad aboard the USS Stribling
1921

The USS STRIBLING
DD-96

The Stribling had sailed for Philadelphia Navy Yard. It took us about two days and two nights if I remember right to go from Charleston to Philly. I was assigned to the forward engine room. I had to check bearing temperatures on the way. I was given a clipboard with a form and I was to read the thermometers every half hour. We stood watches four hours on and four hours off. At last we arrived in the back channel in the Philadelphia Navy Yard.

The Stribling was being changed from a destroyer to a destroyer minelayer and tied up to a dock. We reported aboard and was assigned to our respective divisions. I was assigned to the boiler division.

Our boilers were shut down and they had a small auxiliary boiler out on the dock, supplying steam to the ship to heat water for galley use, etc. so I was put on that job. I had to work four hours on and then I was given eight hours off.

Of course, I had it all to learn because I did not know anything about boilers; in fact I don't believe I had ever seen one before. This auxiliary boiler was fired by coal. After some instructions from time to time I soon got the hang of it.

In the gang on the Stribling was a fellow by the name of Connors. Connors was a big ugly brute. He looked like a big bully. When I first seen him I thought to myself here is a guy who will probably beat the hell out of me. I knew within reason I could never whip him as big as he was. However, he turned out to be one of the nicest guys I have ever known.

Connors had quite a background. He had spent a lot of time at sea. He was in the Merchant Marine when the war started in 1914 and was shipping out of New York to Liverpool. While in Liverpool on a trip he got drunk and when he sobered up he was in the British Army. He was sent down to Asia Minor – Mesopotamia and was wounded there and sent back to England to be hospitalized. While he was recuperating he met one of his old shipmates from the Merchant service. He went aboard the ship with his shipmate and signed on deserting the British Army. When we got into the war he enlisted in our navy and was assigned to a destroyer.

We had established a destroyer base in Queenstown, Ireland. His destroyer was one of the ships sent there. While in Queenstown someone who knew him in the British Army saw him and turned him in to the British Authorities. He said he hurried back to his ship. However they located him. Then it became a legal hassle. In the end he stayed with the U.S. Navy, but was put on probation for a while. He did not get an honorable discharge. I would not have believed this had I not seen his papers.

While we were there it was real summer (July) and hot and humid, but our liberty uniform was dress blues (wool).

While ashore one day it was exceptionally hot and I perspired until my liberty card got soaked. I also had small penknife in the same pocket. The cardboard liberty card and the metal knife came in contact with one another. When walking the knife defaced the name on the card. A few days later I was called up to report mast. The captain presented the card to me and asked for an explanation. After I explained, he ordered another card issued to me.

Before he spoke to me he talked to the man on my right. He stepped in front of the man and said, "What is your name?" The man replied, "Cole". The Captain said, "I want your real name". The man said, "Lothrope sir." The captain said, "Lothrope, you enlisted in the navy in 1913 and after one year of service you left. You were inducted into the U.S. Army in 1917. You served honorably and your unit was cited for exceptional service. Now you are back in the Navy. Due to that army service and honorable discharge from the army I am authorized to place you under one years probation". That evening he went ashore and I have never seen him since.

While we were in Philadelphia, a friend of mine at the time by the name of Henderson asked me if I would like to go on a blind date. I told him yes so we went to town and met these girls. The one I got was nice looking but she was hungry. We went out to Fairmount Park and she was always complaining at being hungry. I tried feeding her hot dogs, hamburgers because I did not have very much money.

Finally Henderson and his girl went somewhere else. We went to a pretty nice restaurant and got a pretty good meal. After the meal was over and I got the check I saw it was over $5.00 and I only had about $3.50 or $4.00 on me. I wondered what I was going to do. I finally excused myself and went to the men's room.

When I got there I looked around and there was another door. I said to a Negro where does that door lead. He said, "I guess it goes out of doors". Sure enough it did. A sailor never leaves his hat. He always slips it in his trousers waist so out the door I went, around the corner there was a streetcar getting ready to pull out so I got on it and back to town I went. I have always hoped that girl had enough money to pay that bill.

A couple of days later she and Henderson's girl came out to the ship. I was firing boiler and as I had told Henderson the story he went along with me. When she seen me she said to him, that I looked like the guy who stood her up.

Finally we completed our overhaul and was ready to leave the yard. On August 5th, 1921 we left Philly and sailed to Newport, Rhode Island. We spent about three weeks there.

While there I found out we were near Fall River, Mass. I remembered that Sergeant Covo (who I had met at the motor school at Brohl) lived there. I located his address and sent him a letter telling him I was in the navy at Newport. He came down to see me. I visited his home a couple of times while we were there. He had family, mother and sister, he was married before the war, but had no children.

When we got into the war he felt he had to get into it. His wife did not agree and as a result she left him and I understood that after he returned she divorced him. He was a fine man and felt bad about that business.

After leaving Newport we sailed for New York. We spent a week there. We got liberty in two watches. I was in the port watch and drew the first liberty. We were given 72 hours. Then the starboard watch got their 72 hours.

When we left there we went to Yorktown, Va. Where we picked up mines and gave our gunners a few days in the mine school. We were told we were going to the Hawaiian Islands, (Pearl Harbor).

From Yorktown we went to Guantanamo Bay, Cuba where we spent a few days.

One day Connors said to me, "Phillips, I am not going to Pearl Harbor. I am going to jump ship right here." (This was while we were in New York anchored in the Hudson River.)

One day some of the boys saw a rowboat come floating by the ship. It came close enough that they tied on to it. When we sailed we brought it aboard. We had it when we arrived in Cuba. Someone put it in the water and tied it to the guardrail.

We were to sail from there early one morning. The evening before Connors called me aft on the fantail. It was after dark, he and a man by the name of Flinch had their sea bags and hammocks and were getting in this boat. They pulled the boat under the dock out of sight and stayed there until we were well gone. They reported into the base commander. Later someone got a letter from Flinch and they were both in the naval brig in Pelham Bay, New York.

We went on to Kingston, Jamaica and got in early in the morning. Each watch was given three hours liberty. We sailed later in the p.m. Kingston was a nice stopover. They were loading bananas on a ship there. There was a narrow gauge railroad on the dock. They would bring stalks of bananas on cars loaded like cordwood. There was a long line of women carrying those stalks aboard ship, working like ants up one gangway and down the other.

We went on to Panama. We anchored out in the harbor at Colon. We had a few hours liberty there, but I had duty and did not go ashore. I was fortunate to be off duty while passing through the canal. I will never forget looking ahead as we proceeded up the bay to the entrance to the first of the Gatun locks and seeing Old Glory waving at the top of the locks.

There are three locks on the Atlantic side. The Gatun locks raise a ship 85 feet from sea level to the Gatun Lake. I believe they call the distance through the Canal approximately 50 miles. It is very interesting trip. On the Pacific side there are two sets of locks, going towards the Pacific. We came to the Miraflores locks just one step down. Then through a lake, the Miraflores Lake to the San Miguel locks. Two steps down. There we reached Balboa. We tied to the dock there. We got liberty and went over to Panama City a few miles away. It is quite an old city and history has it that it was quite a pirate's hangout in the 17th and 18th century.

At the time the U.S. was dry, but we found liquor very cheap here. Also they sold beer at 5 cents so we enjoyed ourselves.

Some of the boys got a monkey, a small spider monkey. They are not very large and have long legs and tail. These two guys reminded me of Mutt and Jeff. Halroyd was a sort of tall slender fellow. Davork was much shorter and inclined to be chunky. They came aboard with this monkey and they had on what is commonly called a crying jag. They were crying because the monkey wouldn't drink with them. We finally threw the monkey overboard.

We were there a few days, took on fuel, water, etc. A couple of us was standing on the dock, alongside the ship when a Panamanian boy came along eating a banana. We asked him if he could get us some., He said yes so we gave him .35 cents and after a while he came back with a wheelbarrow and a big stalk. I still don't know if he stole the bananas and kept our money or how he got that many for so little. He said he had enough money for them.

When we left Panama we had beer and liquor hidden all over the ship. I had about a dozen bottles of beer, hidden in the after boiler room. Our fresh water tanks were there along the port side. I tied strings to the necks and hung them in the tanks then clamped the covers back on the tanks.

From Panama we put in at Salina Cruz, old Mexico on the Gulf of Tehuantepec. We went in there to refuel, but international law would not let us stay there but 24 hours so we did not get far from the ship. The Mexicans there were still more or less mad at us over the Vera Cruz Affair.

We took on oil (fuel) by gravity from some tanks up on a nearby hill (About two miles away). We sent a man up there with the oil company representative to check on the reading on the tank. We had to send an armed guard with him. We had to do the same thing when we took the reading after filling our tanks. We had to work all night refueling.

From Salina Cruz we sailed on to Magdalena Bay, Old Mexico. We stayed there 24 hours also, but we did not get ashore. We anchored out. It was in Magdalena Bay we saw the largest turtles I have ever seen. They floated around that bay like large washtubs. I'll bet some of them would weight 300 pounds.

Some of the gang paid a Mexican $1.00 to get one. He put his boat along side of a big fellow and some way he flipped the turtle into the boat on his back. He butchered it for us and we ate it. (Not too good.)

We turned to – in other words we cleaned the ship from stem to stern. We were there only about 12 hours. Finally we went on to San Diego where we tied up to a buoy alongside destroyers of the 36th destroyer division.

I must mention that on this trip I met a chief machinist mate by the name of Boust. He came to the Stribling while in the navy yard at Philly, but he left us in San Diego. More on him later.

Most of our officers left us in San Diego. Our Captain, Lieutenant Commander Woodside left the ship. We got a new man by the name of Farquihar. He had been a Commander "war time" but reverted back to Lieutenant Commander after the war.

There was an old cruiser, the "Charleston" which was flagship, destroyer division Pacific Fleet. I believe the admiral's name was Eberle. At any rate he did not miss anything and he was a stickler for regulations. He could see us with a long glass when we went to quarters every morning, especially the Black gang as us engineers were called.

We would go to quarters in just anything. We did not try to get in clean uniforms, just our work clothes. After Farquihar came aboard he sent word that he wanted the bunch of pirates on the Stribling put in uniforms.

I don't know why we stayed in San Diego as long as we did, about 5 or 6 weeks. While we were there we had a problem with a fellow in the gang who would hardly ever take a bath. He commenced to smell. We all complained to each other about it until we thought it would be a good idea to give him a bath. His name was Perry. We had all told him he should bathe, but he would always say he would. One night we got our heads together and decided to bathe him. He was on the 4 to 8 watch. After he came off watch he started to climb in his bunk. (We had bunks on the Stribling) without taking a bath so we told him to go bathe first. He said he would take a bath when he was ready. We told him he was ready and we took him. Well it was quite a battle while it lasted. Finally we got him down. Someone got a line and we tied his hands behind him. We finally got him out on topside. We emptied a gear locker (a locker where cleaning gear was kept, made of heavy gauge wire.) We got his underwear off, locked him in there and turned the salt-water hose on him with about 75 pounds of pressure. It did not take long for that to quiet him down. Then we used sand and canvas and a Ki-Yi (scrub brush) on him. When we turned him loose there was no more fight left in him.

He headed right for the Captain's cabin with no clothes on, but one of the other officers seen him first. The captain heard the commotion out in the passageway and came out. He asked Mr. Kell what was wrong. Mr. Kell told him, "It seems as if the gang gave Perry a bath." The Captain told him to get out of there; if the gang had to give him a bath he must have needed it. He sent Kell to inspect his locker, bed and clothes. They disposed of his bedding and Kell made him wash all of his clothes before he could turn in. They gave him new bedding. He went ashore in San Diego the day before we sailed for San Francisco and we did not see him for a while.

The Battleship California had just been placed in commission and came into San Diego. She had some civilian yard workers aboard so we picked them up and took them back to Mare Island Navy Yard. We had a boiler go bad on us so we went into Mare Island and picked up new tubes for it.

I don't remember the date we sailed for Pearl Harbor, but we were seven days in route. That was the roughest seven days I have ever experienced. At one time there was sixteen hours we could not relieve the boiler room and engine room watches. It was too rough to open the hatches.

When we left Mare Island the captain told us that there were five destroyer mine layers in Pearl Harbor and only one of them had completed the trip on her own fuel. The other four had to be towed as much as 600 miles. He said, "We don't want that to happen to this ship. You get us out there on our own and you won't regret it." We did, but we were darned uncomfortable doing it. We just about had enough water to drink. No air circulating fans and a bare minimum of lights. We steamed on one boiler under natural draft. When we got tied up along side the Ingraham we still had about 300 gallons of oil. We almost stripped the stanchions off the bow of the Ingraham getting alongside. The oil barge was waiting when we got tied up so our fires would not go out. 300 gallons was less than an hour's fuel even on auxiliary.

We arrived off Honolulu on the evening before Thanksgiving 1922. Our supply officer and chief commissary steward went over to the town and got the makings for Thanksgiving dinner.

We had two Negro cooks aboard so they got started getting dinner the next morning. They made turkey dressing and baked some of it in large tubs. After they took the dressing from the turkeys, they must have put that in the tubs to keep it warm while they cut up the turkeys. After heating the dressing they sat the tub on the tile deck of the galley.

In the meantime we got under way for Pearl Harbor a few miles up the bay. The bay was a little choppy and this tub started sliding across the deck. Some way or another it must have almost hit one of the cooks on the leg or foot. Both cooks were barefooted because it seems as if he jerked his leg up and became unbalanced and stuck his foot in the hot dressing then in trying to get it out he got the other foot in. Well we had no dressing for that dinner. Captain Farquihar was sure mad, and said he would get rid of those guys and he did. He got two Filipinos in their place.

The USS Stribling DD-96 in the Panama Canal
1921

We were assigned to mine squadron 2, Pacific Fleet. Our flagship was the old Baltimore. Captain Sexton, a four striper, was our boss. The old Baltimore had quite a history, she was at the battle of Manila Bay and had a patch on her bow where a Spanish shell had punched a hole. She had also laid mines in the North Sea with the North Sea mine laying fleet during World War I.

Our duty in the islands was uneventful. We practiced laying mines around Maui, Lahaina etc. In the meantime a supply ship Vega came in and who came in on her but our good friend, Perry. He said he followed us up the coast from San Diego and after we left Mare Island he reported in. They gave him 90 days in the brig and then sent him back to the ship.

In 1922 the Kellogg-Briand Pact went into effect and the Stribling, along with two others, was ordered decommissioned. There were six minelayers there and three were decommissioned. It took us about 60 days to really lay the ship up.

They had an old Spanish-American War troop ship tied up to the dock for a receiving ship. We stayed aboard her until we could get transportation back to the states.

Finally the old army transport Thomas came in and we returned to the states on her. This ship was on this route for many years carrying military personnel from the states to the orient and back.

So there were 700 of us from Pearl Harbor. We arrived in San Francisco the 14th July 1922 and were sent to the receiving ship Boston on Goat Island. Two days later a division of destroyers came in and picked us up for further transfer to the battle fleet. At the time the battle fleet was operating out of Puget Sound, Bremerton, Port Angeles and Seattle, Washington.

We arrived in the bay at Port Angeles. A few other guys and myself was sent to the Mississippi for further assignment. I was aboard the Missy for almost a month.

The first radio I ever saw was a hook up by a first class electricians mate we had on the Stribling. One evening while at Pearl Harbor he got it working and by using earphones we could hear singing and music from Honolulu seven miles away. We all thought it was wonderful.

THE USS IDAHO
BB-42

While on the Missy we could not get paid. Our records were lost and we had not been paid for about a month. Since our records were lost they did not know quite what to do with us. The Missy went to Seattle and we wanted to go ashore so we asked the executive officer for shore liberty. He told us we could not have liberty.

The captain of the Missy was a Captain Jackson. It seems as if Mrs. Jackson (the captains wife) was aboard and she happened to be in the executive officer's office when we asked for liberty so she came out and went aft to the officer's area.

Real soon after that a messenger called us and told us to report to the Executive's office. The Captain himself was there. He told us we could have weekend passes. Later I found out that Mrs. Jackson ran the ship when she was aboard. I met a man who knew the Jackson's personally.

The Missy was ordered to the Navy Yard Bremerton, Wash. so we left her in the yard and went aboard the California. We only stayed on her overnight when she sailed for Port Angeles. There we found our home. Our records had been found and we were permanently assigned to the U.S.S. Idaho.

I will never forget the first few days on the Idaho. I had been used to a small ship where everyone knew each other. We were more like a family on the Stribling. It was like people living in a small town. One could lay anything down and no one would think of taking it. Also when we were away from the high-ranking brass regulations were not so strict.

The Stribling carried a crew of about 275 people, but on the Idaho, a large ship with lots of people there was a lot of difference. If you did not keep your eyes on your equipment it would be gone. We had to change from work clothes (dungarees) to undress uniform for meals. Sometimes dress blues. In warm climates undress whites. Every Saturday A.M. there was either bag inspection or hammock inspection. We had no bunks on the Idaho.

The Idaho had a crew of 1200 sailors, 75 marines and about 50 officers.

I went aboard the Idaho about the middle of September 1922. On the first of October I was assigned to mess cook, waiting tables, washing dishes, tables, benches, etc. For this duty we were paid $5.00 a month extra. Also on payday I would put a mess bowl on the table for contributions. I waited on 20 men, two tables with 10 men to each table. Now each man was supposed to feed the kitty $1.00 on pay day and they usually did. Oh, sometimes there would be a cheapskate who wouldn't. We were paid the 5th and 20th each month. It did not take long to get his number.

I really hated the job at first, but became used to it, and it was not too bad. The worst job was Fridays when we would have to take our tables and benches topside and holy stone, sand and canvas them. I also had to hose them down with salt water. This made them bleach out and get very clean. I was only supposed to have this job three months, but when it was my turn to be relieved I elected to stay another three months.

U.S.S. IDAHO

USS Idaho BB-42   1922

One reason I elected to stay was that we had a chief machinist mate in the engine rooms called Wild Bill Mueller. I had served there with him in center engine room the first two weeks aboard the ship.   There   were   three   engine rooms in the Idaho with a smaller engine room both port and starboard of the center. They were called Port and Starboard engine rooms.

When I first went aboard I was assigned to the main or center engine room and this was my assignment as long as I stayed on the ship. I had heard that Wild Bill was being transferred to the Pennsylvania so I stayed on as mess cook. Besides the pay was good.

Wild Bill was a guy hard to get along with. He was a good engineer, but he had his pets. If he took a liking to you, you could do no wrong and you could get every favor. If it was the other way your life was hell. Nearly every time he went ashore he would come back and show he got into a fight and someone would beat hell out of him.

Mess cooks had to stand quarters every morning at 8:00 a.m. in their respective assigned stations. As the center engine room was mine I had to report there each morning. Imagine my surprise one morning when who should show up but my friend Boust. He was taking Wild Bill's place.

After quarters was over he asked what I was doing? I told him I was mess cooking. He asked how long I had been at it. I told him almost five months. He asked if I wanted to get off of mess cook. I told him I would stay until the end of the quarter, April 1st. He asked me if I would like to stay in the engine room. I told him I believed I would like that very much. Good he said. I would like to have you so on April 1st I went back to the main engine room.

My engine room assignment was boiler feed pumps at first. Then from time to time I took other jobs until when I left the ship I was well acquainted with every part of all three engine rooms.

I believe we had four chief machinist mates. One warrant machinist. A warrant machinist ranks just higher than machinist mate and lower than an ensign and Lieutenant Jr. grade The Lieutenant Jr. grade was mostly in charge of engineer personnel. He had very little to do with engineer duties.

On the 1st July 1923 I was promoted to fireman 2nd class. On April 1st. 1924 I was made machinist mate 2nd class.

In the meantime in Jan. 1923 we went to Panama. On the way down we had battle practice and maneuvers. We then came back to southern California in March for long range firing. After that we went up to San Francisco for a couple of weeks visit before going to Puget Sound for the summer. In November we went into the navy yard for over haul before going back to southern California (San Pedro) for Christmas.

In Jan 1924 we sailed for Panama. The battle fleet consisted of the following battleships, California ("Flag"), Arizona, Pennsylvania, Oklahoma, Tennessee, New Mexico, Idaho, West Virginia, Colorado, Maryland, and Mississippi. Oklahoma, Arizona, Pennsylvania (10–14 inch guns). California, Tennessee, New Mexico, Mississippi, Idaho (12- 14 inch guns). Maryland, Colorado, West Virginia (10–16 inch guns). We had numerous destroyers also some of the Omaha class cruisers, submarines and supply ships. This time we were headed for the Atlantic to meet the Atlantic Fleet. I don't off hand remember the names of all the battleships in the Atlantic Fleet but the Nevada was one of them. Boat racing was one of the main sports along with boxing and football in the navy at the time. The Idaho had the best times in the Pacific Fleet. The Nevada was supposed to have the best time in the Atlantic fleet.

We met them just off Culebra in the Virgin Islands. The Nevada immediately challenged us to a race. We accepted and they sent us word that had $10,000 to put up for their team. We also accepted that wager and went on to beat them by eight boat lengths.

We were at Culebra in Feb and the weather was beautiful. The island has one of the nicest beaches I have ever seen. The land forms sort of a half circle and the sand was as white as snow. One can wade out for almost a half mile in the breakers. You can see the bottom in 50 ft. of water.

When we left there we headed for New York City. However we stopped in at San Juan, Puerto Rico, overnight having gotten there in the afternoon. After we left there we went on to New York City.

We stayed there about a week. I got ashore several times. One day a lad by the name of Benny Tate and I was ashore and we were looking for a place to eat. There was a sightseeing bus at the corner. I asked the driver where we could get a good meal. He asked us if we liked sauerkraut. We assured him we did. He directed us to a place where they served nothing but kraut. One day it was kraut and spare ribs. The next it was kraut and pigs knuckles. When you went in the place you paid .40 cents then sat down to a table and they brought on the food. You could eat all you wanted for 40¢. They served a big plate of kraut, pork, two slices of bread, butter and either coffee, tea or milk or near beer. Remember this is 1924 and we still had prohibition, good beer was not to be had. We were on a 72-hour liberty so we had a room out on 125th street. The next morning we met another shipmate by the name of Hinkle so we took him there for dinner.

The Ziegfeld Follies were running then so we thought we would like to see the Follies. We went over there and saw the prices, figured up our assets between us and found out that between us we did not have enough money for even one ticket. We went across the street and seen Abie's Irish Rose for one dollar and a quarter a seat. It was real good.

It was about the middle of March 1924 when we left there. We went back to Culebra. It was zero weather in New York. When we got back to Culebra it was in the 90 degrees and we went swimming every day when we were off duty.

We went on back through the canal to the Pacific side and started for California. We saw the Arizona pull out and return to Panama. We found out later they found two stowaway "girls" on her. They had been aboard since leaving New York. They were turned over to the American authorities in Panama. I don't know what happened to them or who ever helped them stow away.

After returning to California we had short range firing. Then we went to the Guadalupe Islands, but did not get ashore. We were close enough to see the famous sea elephants however. They are huge ugly creatures.

We followed the same pattern the summer of 1924 – San Francisco, Puget Sound and Bremerton navy yard.

We went back to Panama in Jan. 1925. In March I took the examination for Machinist mate 1st class. When I told the engineer officer I was not going to ship over he said he could not rate me 1ˢᵗ class but if I would ship over I would get the rate as I had passed the examination.

The fleet was scheduled to sail for Hawaii then on to Australia on the 15ᵗʰ of April. We went to San Francisco and they were to sail from there.

There was to be a smoker (boxing matches) in the Civic Center and a baseball game at the Presidio and I was assigned to the rooting party to go to both places. Our machinist in charge was named Ward. I went to him and asked to be excused from both parties. He bawled me out and told me I had better be there because we would be checked in. I went to the smoker and Boust happened to be the one who checked our gang in. I told him I sure as hell did not want to be there. He said O.K. I'll check you in and also check you for the ball game so I took off.

On the 14ᵗʰ of April I made up my bag and hammock and put it outside the executive officer's office door. I was not there for quarters and Boust knew I was being paid off. Ward came by and saw me. I was in dress blues. He stopped and said, "Are you getting paid off?" I said, "Yes sir" he said, "Why don't you ship over'. I said, "Mr. Ward I asked you for a favor the other day and you refused." He looked at me kind of funny, shook his head and started off. Then turned around and came back. I thought he was going to bawl the hell out of me, but he said, "What are you going to do on the outside?" I told him I was going to try to find a job. He said, "I'll get you a letter of recommendation." He did, and I still have it.

A little story about Ward. One time I was in the Pacific Electric station in Los Angeles when I seen him sitting on bench. I walked over and said, "Hello Mr. Ward." He looked at me. He was in civilian clothes. He knew me and said, "Hello Phillips, will you see me home?" I said, "Back to

180

the ship?" He said, "No, I live here in town when I am ashore". Here is my card and address." I seen he was drunk and getting worse. He felt around his clothes and finally found a card. I got him home. He lived out near Hawthorne. When we got to his place it was an apartment house and he lived on the first floor. His first name was Jim. When I rang the bell the door opened a little and a woman, his wife said, "Is that you Jim?" I said, "Yes, Jim is here". She opened the door and said, "Come in here you drunken SOB." She dragged him in and shut the door. She did not ask any questions. This was Saturday night. Monday A.M. he came down in the engine room while we were at quarters. After quarters I noticed him talking to the guys. Finally he came to me. He said, "Did you take me home Saturday night". "No," I said. "It was early Sunday morning." Then he asked me all about it. I did not mention that she had called him a drunken SOB but I guess it was not necessary as I imagine she had called him that before. I showed him the taxi bill and explained what had happened. He reimbursed me and thanked me.

One day I had the auxiliary watch when two new Ensigns, one by the name of Birtchie, and the other I have forgotten, came down to the engine room. They presented themselves and I took them around and explained things to them. Mr. Birtchie became our division officer. He turned out to be a very nice fellow. Thirty years later as a captain he was Bob's commanding officer, as Commandant of Treasure Island Navy Base.

Another time we got a new bunch aboard and one of them was made division officer. One Saturday we were at inspection on the foc'sle (or forecastle). Everyone was in his best dress blues lined up waiting for the captain to inspect us. Our division officer was standing in front of us at attention when a seagull flew over and splattered him just as the captain approached us. The stuff hit the edge of his cap and ran down the side of his face, down over the side of his uniform.

We all wanted to laugh, but as we were at attention we knew better. Our Captain's name was Crowsley and he was rather stern. I don't believe I ever seen him laugh, but when he seen that he had a big smile. He looked the man over and told him he was excused, and that he was not a real sailor until he had been baptized as such.

There are two incidents that occurred while I was on the Idaho that I feel I must relate.

Every summer before we went north to San Francisco and Puget Sound we would have short-range battle practice. This would usually take place on the San Clemente Islands between Los Angeles and San Diego.

One time we were out at practice and I thought I would watch. Engineers have no part in gunnery aboard a battleship. The ship was firing 5-inch guns. The marines had a couple of guns assigned to them. I went up on the gun deck and was standing behind a gun watching. The gun had fired and the shell man had rammed the projectile home. The powder was in bags. The 5-inch guns did not use fixed ammunition at the time.

The powder man rammed home the powder bag. When it was noticed that there was fragments of smoldering bag laying in the lock grooves of the gun breach. The breach man slammed the breach closed just in time, just an instant before the gun fired. Had that new powder bag ignited before the breach was closed some of us would have been killed even as far back as I was, about 15 feet.

A backfire on the Mississippi caused the death of 48 men in June 1924.

There was the California, Mississippi, New Mexico and Idaho in that order. We were firing. Now all these ships had 12–14 inch guns, 4-3 gun turrets. They were firing individual turrets then a broadside. In other words the California would fire three guns in #1 turret and then #2, #3, and #4. Then she would fire a broadside, all 12 guns at once, all over the port side.

It came the Missy's turn to fire. When she fired the broadside there was an explosion on #2 turret. The guns were referred to as #1-2-3 in each turret beginning on the starboard side. #1 gun on #2 turret fired o.k. There was a flash of fire came out of the turret around the gun. #3 gun did not fire. The ship pulled out of line. I have never found out what happened, but every man in the turret and all the way down to the handling rooms was burned to death. They were very lucky the fire did not reach the magazines. This ammunition was also loose, separate projectile, powder bags, etc. It was generally thought a burning fragment of bag was still in the bore, when the powder bag was inserted.

I received my discharge from the Navy on April 14, 1925 and went ashore at pier 26, San Francisco.

End Note

Another tale that Dad told related to the first days after they crossed into Germany after the Armistice. Apparently soon after they hiked into Trier, Germany they came upon a small warehouse. After breaking in they found it to be completely full of brand new German Luger pistols. They were still in the wooden boxes and were still packed in Cosmoline. There were 7mm, 8mm and 9mm pistols in the lot. From what he said there must have been thousands of them because the warehouse was stocked all the way to the rafters with them. Naturally every soldier had to grab several for souvenirs. Little did they know that they would have to hike practically the whole breadth of the country before their tour of duty was to end. Dad said that a two pound pistol may seem light when you pick it up but when you have carried it all day it feels like it weighs 25 lbs. Needless to say there were 7, 8 and 9mm Lugers scattered for many miles along the Moselle River Valley and none that he ever knew of wound up back in the States.

The winter of 1918 – 1919 was especially brutal for the American Expeditionary Forces in Germany. It turns out that 600,000 people in the United States died of influenza that winter and nearly 10,000 Americans in Germany died also along with many thousands of Europeans. It was very strange that neither Dad nor the fellow that stayed with him or even the Nolte family contracted the flu or even a cold that winter. Dad always attributed this to the hot wine that Mr. Nolte gave them every morning. I'm not sure that there is any scientific data to prove this to be true but Dad always believed it.

Dad truly fell in love with the Navy. I suppose this had a lot to do with the fact that he was able to learn more in that job than he had ever been able to in any previous position. In later years when he was in a story telling mood it was generally Navy stories that he would tell.

Book Five

Civil Service

1925 - 1955

CIVIL SERVICE
1923

In Jan. 1923 we made our usual trip to Panama. When we got back I got a letter from my sisters informing me that Mr. Dauner had committed suicide. He had shot himself. I often wonder why he waited so long, but he was a man who could not stand reverses. If everything did not please him or go as he thought they should he would be hard to get along with.

I don't know what happened, in fact the girls did not know. Annie was about 19 and Lizzie, or Elizabeth, was about 17 at the time. He had sold the old place and had bought a little place in another part of town. It was all clear and after a year, as soon as Elizabeth was 18 they got the deed.

When I got out of the navy I decided to go back there. I had no desire to go back to Cimarron to work. I felt I could do better.

In the meantime Annie had left Lawton and was working in Kansas City, Mo. Elizabeth had rented the house partly furnished and was working part time and boarding with some friends. I stopped in K.C. and visited Annie. When I got to Lawton Elizabeth and I decided to take over the place and set up housekeeping. The tenants were leaving anyhow, but first I had come out of the navy with about $800. Upon investigation I found out that taxes had not been paid on the place since the old man died so I brought them up to date. The house had never been wired for electricity so I took care of that. They had been using coal oil lamps all those years.

Work was not plentiful but I did manage to eek out a living. I got the idea of trying to get into Civil Service. There was an opening for boiler fireman at the army post at Fort Sill. I went out to see about it and was informed I would have to take a civil service examination. They also gave me the necessary papers to fill out and told me to watch the bulletin board in the post office.

I found what I thought to be a good position in July 1925. There was an opening for 3rd class engineer at Scott Field, Ill. so I put in for it. I passed easily. I received a grade of 87% and with 5% for military service I had 92% total. I was informed that they picked a man for the job who lived near there and had a little better grade.

About six months later I received a letter from the Veterans Bureau asking me if I would accept a position at Jefferson Barracks, Mo. at $1320 a year. I was not making that much in Lawton so I accepted.

We rented the house. We sold a lot of the furniture to a second hand man. We should have sold it to an antique dealer, as most of the pieces were antiques.

Elizabeth went to live with Annie and I reported in to the Veterans Bureau at Jefferson Barracks, Mo. Elizabeth did not stay with Annie very long. She went back to Lawton and married soon, probably 1926.

At the Veterans Hospital in Jefferson Barracks I was given charge of the boiler plant. I also acted as chief engineer when the chief was gone. The chief was Chris Orf. He was a fine man. At first I was not given very many responsibilities but after I proved to Mr. Orf that the navy trained well he turned more and more over to me.

There were two men in the gang who had been there a couple of years before me. I wondered why they had not been given the responsibility, but after being there about six months I knew. They did not seem to want to accept the job and responsibility that went with it.

There was lots of girls working there in different departments. Those of us who were single were required to live on the station, and were charged $40 a month for room, board, and laundry. I started going out with a girl who worked in the laundry. Her name was Rena Haile.

I finally saved up enough money to buy a 1926 Ford Model T, Roadster. I was proud of that car. I have never had a car since I thought more of.

Well eventually, Rena and I decided to get married. We felt we could easily live on the $80 we were paying for board. Also I had gotten a raise. On September 10th, 1927 we drove down to Hillsboro, Mo and got married, in the courthouse by a Methodist preacher. She said she did not want to be married by a justice of the peace and I was not too fond of the idea either. We had no honeymoon as such. Rena had a sister living in the city. Her name was Carrie Mosner. She and her husband had a daughter La Vonne. La Vonne later married a man named Bill Jones. Rena's folks lived in Barton County, Mo. Near the Kansas line.

Her father and mother were living at the time. She had five brothers, Owen, Bill, Cleo, Walter, and Guy, two sisters, Lavina and Carrie. The two girls were older than Rena.

We immediately asked for our board money and it was allowed so we rented an apartment and moved ourselves. We rented a house finally and bought furniture. We rented for about six years. Then bought a house at 9914 Lark Ave.,

Lemay, Missouri near where Uncle Lou and Aunt Catherine live now. After we were married about three years Rena's health broke. It turned out to be T.B. She quit work and went to bed. She spent six months in bed. I tried to get a transfer to a drier climate when we found out she had T.B. I even had a trade almost worked out with a guy in Tucson but I listened to our doctor when he told me that she would be better off where she was, than moving her some place else. At any rate on Jan 23, 1933 she died.

In the mean time her father had died and was buried in a small cemetery near Jasper, Mo and that is where we buried her, near her father. We had no children. She was good woman.

Mother was working at the hospital when we met. Dorothy McCaffrey (mother) and I were married on May 9, 1934. The priest in St. Andrews parish parlor married us. Kathleen was 9 years old and Jane was 7. Mother and I spent a few days in Hannibal, Mo, on our honeymoon. We moved then to Lark Ave.

We were married only six months when we received a letter asking if I would accept a position as engineer at Whipple, Ariz. At a Salary of $2000 a year with moving expenses paid. It also included a promotion to 1st class engineer. As a 2nd class engineer I was getting $1860 at the time. I told mother I had been offered a raise, but we would have to go to Arizona to get it. She said, "OK."

We had just built a new room on our house for the girls and they only used it about a week when we left. Our transfer was effective Nov. 1, 1934. The V.A. packed and crated our stuff and shipped it by rail.

We had a 1930 Chevrolet coupe, with a rumble seat. We loaded it up and took out for Arizona. The first day we got to Rena's brother Cleo's place in western Missouri. The second day we went to El Reno, Okla., the third day Clovis, New Mexico, the fourth day to Deming, New Mexico. The fifth day we made it to Wickenburg, Ariz. and the sixth day we arrived in Whipple before noon.

They had a house available on the station for us so we moved in. The house was furnished. When our stuff arrived we put it in a shed near the house.

We found the crew here was swell people and we knew we would like our new station. My boss was a man by the name of Bill Fisher. He was a good man, but he liked to go on a periodical drunk ever so often.

Well, he chose to go on one right after I arrived. I had not been there long enough to get acquainted with many of the people or the station so I had a rough time for a while. The boys told me that the man I had replaced would always look out for Fisher and sober him up. I told them I had not gotten him drunk and I would not sober him up. When Bill came back he was as mean as a bear with a sore tooth. He started to tell me how the fellows would work with him to get him sober. I told Bill that if he wanted to get drunk that was his business. He could get as drunk as he wanted and stay drunk as long as he wanted and that I would never interfere. After that he would take two or three weeks leave and leave town. I could always tell when he had been drinking, but I never let him get away with anything.

We were living in a small frame house on the north end of the station then. On March 29, 1936 Bob came along.

The House at Whipple, Arizona

He was born in the old Mercy Hospital in Prescott, on Sunday morning. We name him Robert Alfred.

Our boiler plant was an old antiquated affair. Eight coal burning hand fired boilers. We had hard water so we had lots of hard work. The station at one time was primarily a T. B. Hospital and was scattered all over the place. Some of the building were nearly one half mile from the boiler plant, making heating expensive. We had about five miles of steam lines.

At one time the station had a capacity of 900 beds. But plans were being made to renovate the station build a new main hospital building and bring the wards closer together.

Some of the buildings were old army barracks, but were good solid structures so they were converted over to wards, etc.

In the process of revamping the station they decided to remove the frame buildings. The house we were living in was one of them. We were given a better place near the center of the station. This was Aug. 1st, 1938.

On Jan 3, 1939 while working in the plant I fell from a ladder in the boiler house and broke my right leg. It was felt that I should be sent to a V.A. hospital were there was a good orthopedic surgeon. I was sent to the V.A. hospital at Sawtelle in west Los Angeles. It took me five months to get straightened up and back to work.

On June 10, 1940 Bill Fisher died. He was to go on annual leave, then retire. Another man came in to replace him, a big guy by the name of Welch. He was lazy so I was worse off. Later he and a man by the name of Stiegers traded jobs. Welsh went to Amarillo, Texas. Stiegers was an old man so I had to carry him so he could retire. When Stiegers left I got his job.

In the meantime both of our girls got married. Kathleen was married to Paul R. Jackson of Detroit, Mich. on October 25, 1947. Less than a year later, on September 9, 1948, Jane was married to Thomas M. Robbins, a native of Prescott.

I was commencing to think of retiring and decided I would like to live where I could farm and raise a lot of our living. I got a chance to go back to Missouri. There was a new hospital opening in Poplar Bluff, Mo.

I got that station. It was brand new with up to date equipment. It was nice to have good material to work with; however it was like all new things, there are always a lot of bugs to straighten out.

We arrived in Poplar Bluff on December 15, 1950. We bought two acres near town. We raised about everything we needed and sort of built the place up.

On December 1, 1955 I retired after nearly 36 years of government service. 22 months in the army, 4 years in the navy and 29 years and 6 months with the V.A.

Finally we decided we were getting to the age when we should be nearer our children.

In the meantime Bob had put in a cruise in the navy, came out and married Ann Roberson, a St. Louis girl, and moved to Scottsdale, Arizona so we sold out in Missouri and moved back to Prescott.

You children know the rest. I hereby rest my case. I have tried to tell the story as I remembered it. I am not exactly proud of my past. I feel as if I should have done better. Men who have had no more than I, have gone farther and accomplished much more.

Now all of you can live your own lives and write your own stories. In closing I must tell you all I am much more than proud of all of you.

Love to you all,

Dad

Book Six

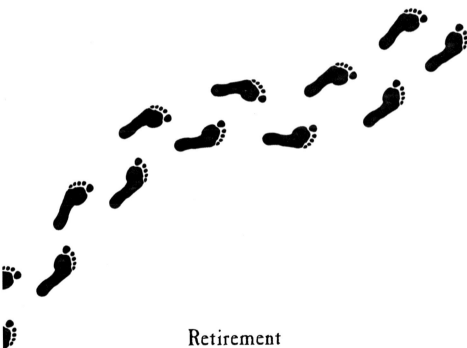

Retirement

1955 - 1987

Dad & Mom's House in Poplar Bluff, Missouri

Dad And Mom's House In Prescott, Arizona

NOTES AND INCIDENTAL COMMENTS

Here are a few of the cattle brands of the people I worked for:

Jack Potter	**U**	U Bar
Vesta Bray	**L/Y**	L Slash Y
Henry Jones	**OO**	2 Circle Bar
George Hubbard	**S**	Quarter Circle S
W. T. Hughes	**UU**	U on hip. U on side - cattle. U on shoulder – horses.
Meredith Hughes	**CM**	
My Brand	**W**	Bar W

Although Dad ended his autobiography at this point it was to be that he lived another thirteen years after finishing this narrative.

I will attempt to elaborate on the rest of his life.

End Note

Throughout his life Dad was an inveterate record keeper. In going through his files after he passed away I found a record of his expenses for a family vacation in July 1936 that I thought would be interesting especially in light of the contrast in the cost of living then with respect to today.

Mom wanted to go back to St. Louis to visit her sisters and I suppose to show off her new son. Dad was allowed 30 days vacation per year and they had not been back to visit family for two and a half years. At this time Arizona was considered wild and wooly and many people believed once you reached Texas going west you had to take a stagecoach and fight Indians.

This time was in the height of the depression and even though Dad had to take a 25% cut in salary he still was working. That would have been devastating under normal circumstances however, in those days with so many people unemployed, it was a blessing to have a job at all.

In 1936 Dad bought a brand new Chevrolet 2 door sedan. It cost $630.00 delivered in Prescott. Dad even got to drive it off the railroad car. In 1936 paved roads were a luxury and a great deal of the trip back there was done on gravel (and sometimes dirt) roads.

The family at that time consisted of Dad, Mom, Kathleen (age 11), Jane (age 9) and myself (I was an infant 4 months old). It will be noted that there was no meals or lodging expenses in Missouri. This was true since that was all done with friends and family. The record follows:

GOING

Flagstaff	gas – 8 ½ gal	$2.04
Winslow	oil – 1 qt	$ .32
Holbrook	gas – 4 ½ gal	$1.08
Gallup	gas – 5 gal	$1.25
Las Lunas, NM	gas – 6 gal	$1.23
Albuquerque	gas – 4 gal	$ .84
Albuquerque	oil – 5 qts	$1.61
Santa Rosa, NM	gas – 8 gal	$1.84
Tucumcari, NM	gas – 3 gal	$ .62
Amarillo `	gas – 6 gal	$1.20
Shamrock, TX	gas – 4 gal	$ .76
Weatherford, OK	gas – 5 gal	$ .85
Oklahoma City	gas – 7 gal	$1.33
Oklahoma City	oil – 5 qts	$1.51
Claremore, OK	gas – 5 gal	$ .95
Carthage, MO	gas – 9 ½ gal	$1.49

| Lebanon, MO | gas – 6 gal | $1.17 |

Car expenses –$20.09

GOING (continued)

Rug		$3.75
Meals (Gallup)		$1.38
Supper (Albuquerque)		$1.22
Cabin (Albuquerque)		$2.50
Breakfast (Albuquerque)		$ .55
Dinner (Amarillo)		$1.35
Drinks		$ .20
Cabin (El Reno)		$3.00
Supper (El Reno)		$1.00
Breakfast (Oklahoma City)		$ .51
Dinner (Vinita, OK)		$1.17
Drinks (Tulsa)		$ .30

Miscellaneous expenses -$16.93

Total -$37.02

RETURNING

St. Louis	oil – 5 qts	$1.50
St. Louis	gas – 9 ½ gal	$1.58
Rolla, MO	gas – 6 gal	$1.06
Lebanon, MO	gas – 5 gal	$ .83
Carthage, MO	gas – 5 gal	$ .79
Vinita, OK	gas – 8 ½ gal	$1.67
Oklahoma City	gas – 10 gal	$1.90
Sayre, OK	gas – 8 gal	$1.36
Amarillo, TX	gas – 7 gal	$1.40
Amarillo, TX	oil – 5 qts	$1.50
Tucumcari, NM	gas – 8 gal	$1.76
Santa Rosa, NM	gas – 5 gal	$1.13

| Albuquerque | gas – 7 gal | $1.42 |

RETURNING (continued)

Gallup, NM	gas – 7 gal	$1.75
Winslow, AZ	gas – 5 gal	$1.25
Williams, AZ	gas – 4 gal	$ .96

Car expenses -$21.86

Lunch (Lebanon)	$ .90
Drinks (Tulsa)	$ .50
Dinner (Stroud)	$1.45
Supper (Amarillo)	$1.15
Cabin (Amarillo)	$3.00
Breakfast (Amarillo)	$ .40
Drinks (Santa Rosa)	$ .20
Dinner (Albuquerque)	$1.43
Supper (Holbrook)	$1.92
Cabin (Holbrook)	$2.55
Breakfast (Winslow)	$ .40

Miscellaneous expenses - $13.90

Total -$35.76

End Note

*When Dad broke his leg in 1939 it was very trau-
matic not only for Dad but also for Mom. When he was transferred to Sawtelle Veteran's hospital in Los Angeles Mom had
to sign all the papers giving them permission to amputate his
leg. When he was sent over there it was expected that amputa-
tion would not only be advisable but necessary. He was put in
the amputee ward and only by the grace of God was he assigned to the surgeon that spent hours putting his ankle back
together like a jigsaw puzzle. Although his ankle healed so he
could walk he suffered with a painful and completely locked up
ankle for the rest of his life. I was told that there were 14 breaks
in the ankle.*

*When WWII broke out Dad was one of the first to try to
re-enlist in the Navy. They said that if he could jump up and
down on his right foot they would accept him. He jumped up all
right but when he came down he collapsed and they rejected him.
He almost cried because he so wanted to serve.*

Whipple

After Dad and Mom were transferred to Whipple, Prescott became the family's hometown. It was quite unusual for an employee of the VA to be at the same station for 17 years. Dad was not transferred mostly because he was one of the few people that could supervise operation of the antiquated coal fired boiler plant that they had at Whipple. In the last few years that we were at this station Dad did oversee the installation of a new gas fired plant that was incredibly better and more modern.

Mom integrated into the community and developed many close friends. The list of their friends would fill up many books however there are some people that were very much deserving of mention in this book. I would say without reservation that Leo and Vera Keeney is one couple that needs to be included. Leo worked at Whipple as a painter and Vera had been a schoolteacher in Prescott. They and their daughter, Veronica (she preferred to be called Vicki in later years) were not only close friends but generous to a fault when it came to hunting, fishing or even trying to teach music to a klutz like me. Leo and Vera both were great musicians and music played a major part in their lives. Vera was one of Mom's best buddies.

Another person that it's important to include was Billy Stewart. Billy was a very unusual man. He was a bachelor and one of the most generous people that ever lived. Billy was a world-class marksman with almost any firearm and taught Kathleen and Jane and me to shoot. Billy not only taught my family to shoot but also a great many of the kids in Prescott. He also taught us to drive and to hunt. Billy loved kids and was constantly doing things for the kids of the community. Although he only stood about five feet tall and weighed about 100 lbs. he could play tennis, bowl and pack a deer out of the forest like it was nothing. Billy worked for Dad in the boiler plant and spent a lot of his time with us as a friend to the whole family. I'm sure that one of the reasons that Billy and Dad struck a responsive chord was the fact that both of them had been raised in orphan's homes. Billy once said that his father had gotten in touch with him for the loan of $20 and that he wouldn't send the money because when his father dropped him and his sisters off at the orphan's home the old man walked away and even though Billy's sister was crying the father never looked back. Billy never forgave his father for that and as far as I am aware never corresponded with his father for the rest of their lives.

During the war years (WWII) Prescott was full of interesting characters. One that stands out in my memory was Gus Schraplo. Gus was an old German from the old country and definitely pro-Nazi. When Germany marched in to Poland in 1939 Gus contacted Dad saying how proud he was that the Anschluss (annexation) had begun and how brave the

German Soldiers were. Dad almost exploded. He told Gus that we had to go over and kick hell out of the krauts in 1914-1918 during WWI and we would probably have to do it again. He also told Gus to get away from him and as far as I know they never spoke again. There was also a couple named Short that were associates of Gus. They made no secret of their support for the Germans. They all belonged to the local chapter of the German-American Bund, which was a pro-Nazi organization. They sort of gravitated to Dad because they knew of his German heritage. Although Dad always said he didn't speak German I suspect he understood a great deal more than he was willing to admit. One thing was certain, Dad never liked nor did he ever trust the Germans or the Japanese.

Poplar Bluff

Moving to Poplar Bluff was traumatic for myself since I was ensconced in high school and had my friends and had never lived anywhere else. I must admit I caused Dad a lot of heartaches but looking back it was a good thing since it opened me up to a whole new set of perspectives.

Mom and Dad both adapted rapidly into the community. Dad had the circle of friends starting with work, which later was expanded through his association with neighbors and Mom's friends. Mom had church and through her association with the people there had a very busy social life. As for myself, we had moved there in the middle of the school year so it didn't take long for me to make friends at school and to form a social life of my own.

I believe that the biggest shock of moving to that part of the country was the lack of progress in that area versus what we were used to in Prescott. Poplar Bluff was approximately the same size (approx. 15,000 pop.) as it had been at the turn of the twentieth century. Aside from the Veteran's Hospital the only other major sources of revenue in the town was the International Shoe Factory, the Missouri Pacific Railroad Steam Locomotive repair shops and a cotton gin. This left the economy of the area quite stagnant. When the V.A. built the Hospital they were forced by Federal Law to pay higher salaries for even relatively menial labor than it was possible to earn in the area. Even after the V.A.

moved in the wage for a master carpenter, bricklayer, electrician etc. maxed out at $50 / week. Even in 1950 that was barely a living wage. When the V.A. first started hiring there was a two-mile long queue to apply for jobs.

The people of Poplar Bluff were very clannish in many ways. The V.A. brought in a bunch of "new" people which, at first, were somewhat frozen out of the social fabric of the town. This did not last long partly since the personnel from the V.A. for the most part had lived in new towns for most of their working life and knew how to accommodate themselves into new situations. Mom and Dad lived in Poplar Bluff for 18 years and owned the same house for 17 years. When Dad and Mom decided to move the neighbors threw them a party. One man came up to them and said, "You people are sure going to be missed around here. You were awfully nice for new people." Any family that had not settled in that area prior to the Civil War was considered "new" people.

TYPIST'S COMMENT

Dad,

You have a lot to be proud of. You have led a proud and successful life. Anyone who rears three responsible adults has fulfilled life's major role.

Not everyone was deemed to be famous, if so there would be no glory. It is more important for a man to be famous in the eyes of his family than in the eyes of the world. In our eyes you are one of the greatest.

You may think your accomplishments are minor, but to us they are the greatest possible. If our accomplishments are as great, then God has blessed us greatly and has double blessed you.

Ann
(1974)

End Note

Dad was always working in one form or another, after moving to Prescott Mom and Dad bought a small two-bedroom house at 207 N. Washington St., which they immediately re-decorated and turned into a nice home. There was a ramshackle barn / garage on the back of the property which was shared by the next-door neighbor. This structure irritated Dad no end so the result was that Dad and the neighbor tore it down and rebuilt two identical garages in the same location.

Dad even planted a garden but it was tiny with respect to the garden in Poplar Bluff. It served its purpose though since it was a way for Dad to stay busy.

During these years Dad had several pursuits, among these was enrolling in college. When Yavapai Community College initiated a program that allowed senior citizens to attend and take courses at no charge Dad took advantage of it.

Initially Dad had always wanted to learn Spanish so he took a course in Conversational Spanish.

At first he was very intimidated and he didn't believe he would fit in since he only had eight grades of formal education.

After the Spanish course he decided to take Southwest History. One day Dad found that the book that was being used was incorrect. Dad was absolutely sure because he had lived through the period they were studying.

To put this in perspective I must point out that Dad always put teachers on a pedestal in his own mind and in general believed that they could do no wrong.

After he found the error in the book he agonized for several days before finally pointing it out to the instructor. The instructor was fascinated with Dad's analysis and asked him to lecture the class on what was correct. After this the instructor was the first to ask Dad what was accurate and what was not. Some of the other students thought he was wild and woolly but he was very popular.

During these years Mom decided to take swimming lessons. It was hilarious in a way because Mom was the only lady in the class that could see well enough to open all the other lady's combination locks on the lockers. Unfortunately all of the other ladies also put their false teeth in the lockers and Mom had a terrible time understanding them well enough to get the combinations.

Dad was always available to the family or others if they needed help with a construction project. In fact, he built an out-

house for a Girl Scout camp in the Bradshaw Mountains. For this and I believe other works he was given a plaque naming him an Honorary Girl Scout. He was always quite proud of that.

Dad loved to walk. He would walk all over Prescott just for fun. He would visit with all sorts of friends, especially Orville Bozarth and people he knew up at the Pioneer's Home. He always said that he knew every widow in town.

In the early 1980's Dad started tripping over curbs and falling down. He would never seem to hurt himself and generally had no problem getting back up. He finally saw a Doctor about the problem and was told that, due to hardening of the arteries brought on by old age, the blood supply to his brain was somewhat restricted and he would have to start taking a walker everywhere he went. This was traumatic for him since it would curtail his main form of recreation. He tried carrying the walker with him but that proved to be impractical since when Tommy Robbins looked into it he discovered that Dad was walking from six to eight miles a day.

On May 9, 1984 Mom and Dad celebrated their Fiftieth wedding Anniversary. They had a reception and party at the Sacred Heart Church in Prescott. Many of their friends came in from all over. Some even came from as far away as St. Louis.

About this time Paul and Kathleen decided that it would be a good thing for Mom and Dad to move in to their house. This was a very generous offer on their part and even though Dad had reservations about losing his independence both He and Mom saw the wisdom in the offer. This proved to be a great solution since that would allow them to have their own apartment and privacy but with assistance always close if needed.

When the house was sold and they were moving out Dad had to give away all his tools, guns and other things that he had accumulated over the years. Moving day was June 7, 1986. On moving day he was practically in tears and he told me that it was tough giving up all the things that he had worked so hard for all his life. He said that it was the first time that he could recall not owning a gun.

Dad passed away on January 17, 1987 a little less than three months short of his 91st birthday. It was ironic that Dad passed away at Whipple where he had worked so many years. He is buried in Prescott.

Except for the last year when health problems started to become a real problem Dad was extremely sharp and never suffered from many of the diseases of old age.

In going through Dad's effects after he passed away we found a note that I will paraphrase as follows:

"Pay all my bills and if there is anything left over have a Party." We had the Party at the Sheraton in Prescott a few months after he passed away and he was toasted liberally.

As it turned out Dad was retired for more years than he worked at the VA. Also, at the time of his passing he was earning more dollars than he had ever earned in his life. This was due to the government giving periodically small 1% raises to the retirees. During these years one of his major regrets was losing all his friends and not having anyone to just BS with. He really missed the friends that could share experiences with him and as was said before, tell...

"The first liar ain't got a chance tales."